I0169531

SEVEN MINUTES IN ETERNITY

WITH THE AFTERMATH

by

William Dudley Pelley

&

Sister Thedra

Copyright © 2021 by Halls of Light, LLC

All rights reserved. This book or any portion thereof may not be reproduced or used in any manner whatsoever without the express written permission of the publisher except for the use of brief quotations in a book review.

ISBN: 978-1-7373071-2-9

Contents

SEVEN MINUTES IN ETERNITY

I

IN THE foothills of the Sierra Madre Mountains near Pasadena, California, I formerly owned a bungalow. When I wanted seclusion in order to complete a knotty job of writing, I laid in a stock of provisions, bade adieu to acquaintances, motored up to this hideaway and worked there undisturbed. My only companion was Laska, a mammoth police dog.

I had come by the bungalow through peculiar circumstances. I cannot ignore them in the light of what occurred.

My life had been an eventful one. Shortly after my birth in Lynn, Massachusetts, my father had entered the Methodist ministry. He had filled pulpits in North Prescott, New Salem, and East Templeton. Then the compensations of a country minister being insufficient to meet the expenses of a growing family, he had moved to West Gardner, Mass., where he entered newspaper work. My earliest recollection of a typecase was in climbing a stool in the office of the *Gardner Weekly Journal* before the Spanish War and setting up my name in composing sticks that were always in demand by much-harassed printers. From Gardner my father moved his family to Springfield. I went through the grammar schools in Gardner and Springfield but after finishing one year in high school he engaged in a manufacturing business in Fulton, N. Y., and there I joined him.

1

I do not propose to intrude an autobiography at the opening of this article on an epochal experience more than to say that I had arrived at a strange interlude in my life when I came into possession of the now-famous bungalow.

I was sixteen years old when I joined my father in his northern New York factory making tissue-paper products. Five years later, on reaching my majority, the business had grown to such a point that I had become General Superintendent of a plant employing 103 men. When unfriendly elements secured control of the concern, freezing father and me from its control, I went into newspaper work. I became feature writer on the *Springfield (Mass.) Homestead,* I was night-man on the *Boston Globe* for western Massachusetts, I founded and ran the *Chicopee Journal*, I sold this first paper of mine to purchase *The Deerfield Valley Times* in Wilmington, Vermont. I sold this second paper to work for Gov. Frank E. Howe on the *Bennington Banner.* While on the *Banner*, I began writing fiction for the national magazines. I was making highly profitable strides as a fiction writer when I bought the *St. Johnsbury Evening Caledonian* in St. Johnsbury, Vt.

I had run the *Caledonian* only a few months when I was solicited by the sponsors of the Methodist Centenary Movement to go to the Orient on a layman's survey of Foreign Missionary Work. When America entered the war, I got into khaki in the Far East, becoming a Red-Triangle man with the troops in Siberia and impromptu consular courier.

The years following the war had not been unprofitable. I had sold my eastern newspaper interests to go to California and make motion pictures from many of the 200 magazine stories and three novels I had produced since leaving the *Bennington Banner*. I made a score of movies in Hollywood and with a Yankee's weakness for engaging in any sort of pursuit that promised profit, I also had interests in a western film magazine, in a chain of west coast restaurants, in a real estate firm, and in an advertising agency.

What I am getting at is, up to October, 1927, I had traveled over half the earth, met all sorts and conditions of men, made and lost several modest fortunes, and reached a point where the mere making of money or reading my name in print had entirely lost its zest. I was spiritually tired. The vigilance of business had begun to pall on me; I felt as if I wanted to get away from everything I had ever been or known and spend a year in study and meditation. I not only wanted to read several shelves of books that I had never found time to read, but I also wanted to *write* some books that I never would be permitted to write as a popular author of modern fiction.

I remember graphically the morning in 1927 when I arrived at my decision. Angered at the petty harassments of business, I had gotten into my car and driven out toward Beverly Hills. As I drove moodily, I turned over in my mind what my life had encompassed up to that moment: little more than an unceasing struggle for money or acclaim. And the irony was, that I didn't want either

I shall have more to say further on in this article concerning some of my reactions to life that had made me the chap I was back there in 1927. However, I shall never forget arriving at the end of a blind road on the far side of Beverly Hills and stopping my car before a sign that read:

BEYOND THIS POINT IMPASSABLE

Go Back!

I stopped my motor and sat staring at the sign. I felt that I had somehow come to the end of another sort of blind road and that the signboard held an allegorical significance. Sitting in the California sunshine off there on that abandoned sandlot that morning, I cast up an accounting with myself.

Beyond this point impassable! Go back!

I decided that I would go back. I would go back and divest myself of all the entangling business alliances that were adding nothing to my peace of mind, I would get rid of the interests that were burning up my spiritual vitality and returning me nothing but dollars. I would stop journeying about America, get all my personal possessions together and put them permanently under one roof where I would settle down in the midst of them and write a few books, not for public consumption, not to pander to popular markets, but to feed my own soul.

I planned out a wholly different mode of living for the rest of my life, sitting there in my motorcar that morning. And when I finally started my engine and swung the machine about, it was to drive back into Hollywood and proceed to put my decision into drastic execution.

I would get as far away from the fleshpots of Hollywood as I could and yet remain in contact with such business interests as I could not wholly dispose of. And to this end, that same afternoon, I headed the machine across into Pasadena and up toward Mount Lowe. Somewhere up in the little unpaved byway streets of the real estate developments that snuggled against the mountain, I felt I would find that which I sought. And an unerring sixth sense seemed to be guiding me.

In late afternoon, with the sun dropping below Catalina Island far out on the west, I turned south from Lake Avenue in Altadena and coasted slowly down Mount Curve Drive. Halfway down the grade I came upon a quaint little English bungalow, a story and a half high, set with a garage behind a row of white birches. It was tenantless, for sale, and open for inspection.

The companion I had with me that afternoon will attest that as I veered my car up its driveway and came to a halt in the rear of the premises, I said: "This bungalow is *mine*! I'm going to live here just as surely as though all my goods were inside this house at this moment!"

The presentiment was overwhelming. In some strange way I seemed to be "remembering forward" . . .

I felt as though the house had been built and left there, waiting for me to arrive at my decision of the morning, twenty miles distant in Beverly Hills.

I was astounded with the case with which I acquired the premises. Within a week I was ensconsed inside it, had begun to furnish it and collect my various possessions from all over the country to make it my permanent abiding-place.

I know now that I had reached a crisis in my life, that morning in Beverly Hills. I know now that there was more than mere spiritual discontent in my decision to cloister myself for a year and do the reading and writing I had always wanted to do, prohibited by secular designs upon my time.

So from October to the following May, I kept the familiar little place as my hideaway and literary workshop. I began the collection of a library. I acquired my big police dog, Laska, as my solitary companion.

During the windy winter of 1927-1928, we lived there in the structure, slowly making it comfortable, subduing the sagebrush and wild poppy in the yard, grading the land and installing a swimming pool for the summer that was coming. . .

I am forced to admit, however, that Laska and I had not spent many nights beneath its roof before I noticed that the dog was ill at ease inside the rooms. She would pace the floors for half-hours at a time, halting in queer places and cocking her steel-shell ears at passageways and corners. Once she awakened suddenly from her place before the hearth in the livingroom, to back away from an invisible something and bring up in a corner of the library bookshelves. There she sat with head aslant *looking at someone or something that seemed to be actually in the intersection of the shelves!* She sat there thumping her tail on the rug, the hair on her neck uneasy, turning from time to time to send me a look of perplexity, and whimper. At other times she would go to the foot of the stairs and give short worried barks up the flight with both paws resting on the lowest step.

Had the bungalow been an old house, I might have thought it haunted. But it was less than six months old and no death had ever occurred beneath its roof. All the same, night after night as I lay in bed alone in the upper story at the back, I heard strange sharp cracks of the boards beneath the stairs as though someone were stealthily ascending. Laska, asleep at the foot of the bed at such times, would spring to her

6

feet and rush out barking. Many a time she would arise, go downstairs in the dark and eternally pace the length of the livingroom.

I never saw anything savoring of the supernatural, however, and was more interested than frightened at the behavior of the dog. Meanwhile I got along with my writing.

HAVING been denied an academic education, I had educated myself, so to speak, ever since the days with father in the factory, by reading in bed for two or three hours every night before I turned off the light. For nearly twenty years I had done this. And my reading had encompassed every solid and substantial subject imaginable. I had an unaccountable interest in history, biography, political economy, and ethnology. No matter where I happened to be, or what the nature of my daily activities, I crammed interminably but without conscious purpose.

I must emphasize here, however, that I was equally *unattracted* to books on comparative religions, the supernatural, or psychical research. I had the layman's inborn aversion to spiritualism, derived from my orthodox parents. Of theosophy I knew nothing and cared even less. Between October and May I did acquire and try to read one of Sir Oliver Lodge's books on survival, but it failed to hold my interest. I had a virgin mind therefore, for all that now happened. . .

Of all subjects that I explored in those twenty years of self-education, history was my *forte*. I felt that I knew world history as I knew my own biography. And yet I had also grown a strange dissatisfaction with general books on history. The histories of the world were a grandiose compilation of battle-dates, superimposed on the aggrandizements of generals and statesmen. Oftentimes I wondered why no one had written a history that should account for the racial, instead of the political, urges of peoples. What was the underlying cause that made one people suddenly pick up their women and children and dogs and chattels and move over into the country of another people, at a cost of great slaughter to both? Was some ulterior influence at work of which historians knew nothing?

I decided to study this problem and write a book upon it. I would write a short history of the world to be called *"The Urge of Peoples"* and tackle the Historical Exposition as no one had ever before attempted.

It was to be a matter of three years before I was to get my cues straight for this great work, but I could not know that at the time. I started to write to "please my soul." It was around the first of May, 1928, that I finally commenced this labor. I still have the pages of manuscript preserved exactly where I left off when the Night of Nights came.

For this thing happened—

THE WORK was going well, I was mentally untroubled, feeling physically fit, writing six to eight hours a day with plenty of outdoor recreation.

For the first time in many years I was having opportunity to browse, ponder, meditate, and study. When I became brain-weary I would whistle for Laska and we would go out for a tramp in the canyon. Or I would clear away more sagebrush on my land and do more grading with shovel and barrow. Nothing in my mode of living, therefore could possibly have accounted for the experience that overtook me. Indeed, I might almost state that in a manner of speaking I had been "turned out to grass" for eight months in order to quiet myself and prepare for the illumination which I now believe was scheduled from the first.

Insofar as I can recollect the time—for I made no particular notation at the date—I had worked up to the 25th or 28th of May. That night I retired around ten o'clock and lay in bed reading until I dozed. The book had nothing to do with what subsequently happened, nor had any occurrence of that day or week or month any special significance in what that memorable night brought forth. I emphasize this fact in order to refute the claims of the skeptical that what I underwent was some form of neurotic psychosis. The book was a notable volume on ethnology, something of a hobby as I have set forth.

In all honesty, however, I must confess that during the evening I had arrived at a crucial point in the writing of *"The Urge of Peoples"* where I had laid down my pen to consider the puzzling subject: *What Were Races?* How did it come about in Nature that one man's skin was black, another's white, another's red, another's yellow? How did it happen that a Chinaman would be a Chinaman for a thousand generations never mind where he lived, or what his environment? How did it happen that an Englishman transferred to the Orient would stay an Englishman though he ate Chinese food and talked the Chinese language till he scarcely knew himself when he looked in a mirror? What was this vast mystery of race, and why down all history were the races so demarked?

Before morning I discovered!

I felt drowsy around midnight, laid the volume on ethnology aside, pulled off my glasses and extinguished the bed-lamp. I had gone through a similar routine on a hundred other evenings; the day had been no different from a hundred other writing days spent at the bungalow.

My sleeping chamber was located at the back of the house and was perfectly ventilated, with two casement windows opening toward the mountains. Laska curled on the floor at the foot of my bed—her accustomed sleeping-place—and that she did not externally motivate the phenomena in any way, I am positive. When it ended and I was back in my body, I stumbled from the bed and my action awoke her, bringing her over beside me where she thumped her tail on the rug and sought to lick my wrist.

I do not recall having any specific dreams the first half of the night, no physical distress, certainly no insomnia. For twenty years I had been an average smoker and puffed my pipe constantly over my typewriter. But I had never observed any derogatory effects from such indulgence and was no more distressed than usual from this particular day's consumption of tobacco.

But between two and four in the morning—the time later verified—a ghastly inner shriek seemed to tear through somnolent consciousness. In despairing horror, I wailed to myself:

"I'm dying! I'm dying!"

What told me, I don't know. Some uncanny instinct had been unleashed in slumber to awaken and warn me. Certainly something was happening to me—something that had never happened in all my life—a physical sensation that I can best describe as a combination of heart attack and apoplexy.

Mind you, I say *physical* sensation. This was not a dream. I was fully awake and yet I was not. I knew that something had happened to either my head or heart—or both—in sleep and that my conscious identity was at the play of forces over which I had no control. I was awake, mind you, and whereas I had been on a bed in the dark of a California bungalow one moment when the phenomenon started, the next I was plunging down a mystic depth of cool blue space not unlike the bottomless sinking sensation that attends the taking of ether for anesthetic. Queer noises were singing in my ears. Over and over in a curiously tumbled brain the thought was preeminent:

"So this is death!"

I aver that in the interval between my seizure and the end of my plunge, I was sufficiently possessed of my physical senses to think: "My dead body may lie in this lonely house for days before anyone discovers it, unless Laska breaks out and brings aid."

Why I should think that, I also don't know—or what difference it would have made to *me*, being the lifeless "remains"—but I remember thinking the thought as distinctly as any thought I ever originated and put on paper in the practice of my vocation.

Next I was whirling madly. Once in 1920 over San Francisco an airplane in which I was a passenger went into a tail-spin and we almost fell in the Golden Gate. *That* feeling! Someone reached out, caught me, stopped me. A calm, clear, friendly voice said close to my ear:

"Take it easy, old man. Don't be alarmed. You're all rights We've got you and are here to help you!"

11

Someone had hold of me, two persons, in fact, one with a hand under the back of my neck, supporting my weight, the other with arms slipped under my knees. I was physically flaccid from my "tumble" and unable to open my eyes at first because of the sting of queer opal light that diffused in the place into which I had come.

When I finally managed it, I became conscious that I had been borne to a white marble pallet and laid nude upon it by two strong-bodied, kindly-faced young men in white uniforms not unlike those worn by internes in hospitals, who were secretly amused at my confusion and chagrin.

"Feeling better?" the taller of the two asked presently as physical strength to sit up came to me and I took note of my surroundings.

"Where am I?" I stammered.

They exchanged good-humored glances.

"Don't try to see everything *in the first seven* minutes!" was all the answer they offered me then.

THEY did not need to answer my question. The query was superfluous. I *knew* what had happened. I had left my earthly body back on a bed in a bungalow in the mountains of California. *I had gone through all the sensations of dying* and whether this was the Hereafter or an intermediate station, most emphatically I had reached a place which had never been duplicated in all of my experience.

I say this because of the inexpressible ecstasy I felt in my new state, both mental and physical.

For I had carried some sort of a physical body into that new environment with me! I knew that it was nude. It had been capable of feeling the cool, steadying pressure of my friends' hands before my eyes opened. And now that I had reawakened without the slightest distress or harm, I was conscious of a beauty and loveliness of environment that surpasses all chronicling on printed paper.

A sort of marble-tiled portico, the place was, lighted by that soft, opal lumination, with a crystal-clear pool in a white stone basin diagonally across from the bench on which I remained for a time striving to accredit just what had transpired. I can best liken the structure to a roofed-in Roman garden about fifteen feet high and thirty feet square. Heavy smooth pillars supported its roof. The illumination came *from the material itself,* a soft alabaster whiteness that scientists in our earth-world would doubtless identify as "cold light." . . .

I had "come down" onto the bench that was set against the west wall. This wall was blank behind me. On my left, to the north, a corridor supported by more of the pillars ran an interminable distance eastward; I could not make out where it went and did not explore it. Across before me, the east wall was unbroken, but at my right the whole south wall was open. Three or four steps led down onto greensward, into a garden that was eerie and indistinct in a sort of turquoise haze. . .

The marble basin opened in the southeast corner of this portico floor; a flight of a dozen steps led down into immaculate water undisturbed by a ripple.

I looked from the garden vista, with its backdrop of turquoise sky, to the two friends who had received me. There were no other persons anywhere in evidence in the first half of my experience. I swung my feet down from the pallet to the floor and sat staring at the two men with my hands grasping the edge of the pallet beside my naked knees.

Somehow I knew those two men, knew them as intimately as I knew the reflection of my own features in a mirror. And yet something about them, their virility, their physical "glow," their strong and friendly personalities – sublimated – kept me from identifying them at once.

Apparently they knew a good joke about me. They continued to watch me with smiles in their eyes. I recall that the older and taller of the two, the one whose hands had been under my neck, *stood wiping his hands upon a towel as he regarded me, as though something had come off my body onto his palms that he wished to be rid of, after touching me.*

At length I found my voice. Looking beyond them and around me, my gaze came to the bench beneath me. I thumped it with my palms. My first words were:

"Great Scott! It's *real*."

"Of course it's real," my friend returned, still smiling.

I got up from my marble bench and moved dazedly about the portico till I came and stood at the edge of the pool.

"Bathe in it," the instruction came. "You'll find you'll enjoy it!"

I went down the steps into the most delightful water. And here came one of the strangest incidents of the whole adventure. *When I came up from that bath I was no longer conscious that I was nude. And the sensation of nudity did not occur to me again throughout my visitation!* On the other hand, neither was I conscious of having donned clothes. The bath did something to me in the way of clothing me. What, I don't know.

But immediately I came up garbed somehow by the magic contact of that water.

IT DID not occur to me to feel either wonder or awe that I had left my physical body and penetrated to this delightful place. It all seemed as natural as it seems natural to me at this present moment to be sitting in this fleshly body again, putting these words on sheets of white paper. Thus it no more occurred to me to discuss the fact that to all intents and purposes I was "dead" than it occurs to me to go about this life discussing the fact that I am "alive" . . . there seems to be only one continuity of life and consciousness and we feel as comfortably at home in one vehicle or environment as in another.

While I had been bathing, the second man who had received me went somewhere outside the portico and I never saw him again. But my first splendid friend stayed with me. Clothed, I sat down again on the pallet and we entered into converse. I did not ask why I had come there. I was not particularly concerned about those I had "left behind" in the earthly state. But the great pertinent fact that I learned that night, and which has since altered my entire conception of life in the world, came out subsequently in our hour's conversation.

The friend who had received me had been in earthly life the scion of an old Southern family who had "gone over" by the accidental discharge of a rookie's rifle in a Southern Army camp in 1917. He had been an officer in that camp and had dropped in his tracks as the bullet entered his heart, dying instantly. Yet, so sublimated in appearance was he, so virile as I have said, so ruddy and stalwart, over what he had been in earth-life, that at first I scarcely knew him. It took us some moments to get acquainted.

Quizzically he asked me: "Don't you remember being here before?"

"When have I ever been here before?" I asked him.

"Countless times," he assured me, smiling more indulgently. "You left this plane or condition to go down into earth-life and function as the person you know yourself to be. Don't you remember *that*?"

"You mean I lived as a person before being born as William Dudley Pelley?"

"Everyone has lived before—hundreds of times before. People still in earth-life will live hundreds of times again—as they may have need of the mortal experiences. It's the very basis for all human relationships."

I pondered this.

"You're writing a book on the peculiarities of earthly races," my friends went on subsequently. "You came to the place where you wondered what races were. I'll tell you what they are. They're great classifications of humanity epitomizing gradations of spiritual development, starting with the black man and proceeding upward in cycles to the white. Each race is an earthly classroom to which people go to get certain lessons in specific things. When they've acquired the experiences from those lessons they come back into this condition and rest, absorbing the increment from those experiences into their characters and thus 'developing' . . . *don't you remember being here before?"*

Now my friend's name in earthly life was William, the same as mine is William. Addressing one another back and forth as "Bill"—as we did – may create some confusion in the reader's mind as to which Bill was speaking. As this same person has been my mentor on the Higher Plane ever since, conversing with me clairaudiently as I will later delineate, I put this explanation here to clarify who is meant by "William" in my later communications. It does not mean any sublimation of myself. . .

I CANNOT print here a literal transcript of all that William and I discussed in the hour that now followed. Humanity is not ready for an exposition of the great fundamentals of human life, steeped as it is in the tenets of orthodoxy and man-made concepts of the "hereafter" . . . if I told the exact truth of what was discussed that night, my whole narrative might be discredited.

But vaguely I knew that I *had* been in that same state prenatally; it was far more familiar to me than mortal environment. I was gradually coming into a sense of recalling something dim and vague in the coffers of Long Memory, when this peculiar thing happened:

All at once I perceived a bluish mist beginning to swirl about me. At first I took it to be hallucination. It seemed that heavy furls of smoke were laving around me, getting thicker and thicker, until they got not only opaque but tangible to the touch.

Suddenly they got so strong and swirled so fast that William's face and figure were blotted out. The thick odorless mist *had actually seized hold of me and I was swirling with it!* Faster, faster, faster I spun in that frightful carousal. Then I lost all sense of sight or identity in the vortex of it. Straight up through the heart of it I seemed to travel at a fearsome pace, to poise abruptly in midair. And as I poised, something awful closed about me! It seemed as though a great suit of clammy, cloying armor, a miasma of implacable sinew, had shut around me. It crunched me horridly, an excruciating agony that ended in a *click!*

I opened my eyes to my California bedroom, with the faint patches of starlight designating the windows! I was back in the mortal thing, the grinding and groaning of atoms, that made up my earthly body! My heart was pounding frightfully; my constricted forehead was sopping wet with perspiration.

I lay stunned for half a moment, striving to accredit the sickening thing that had happened.

I was back in earth-life and I had not wanted to come back. My physical flesh was loathsome to me. I pulled myself up on one elbow in the bed.

Then from somewhere I heard a strangely familiar voice address me. Was it audible in the room, or inside of my head? I did not bother to question. *I only knew it was William's voice and he was crying out to me clearly and distinctly from the Dimension that I had just quitted so queerly:*

"Come on back here, Bill! You and I aren't finished with our visit yet."

"Come back?" I cried aloud. "What do you mean, come back. I don't know how to get back."

"Oh yes, you do," the voice retorted. "Lie back on your pillow. You know the process in the depths of your subconscious. Just relax and *come!*"

I make the solemn affidavit, that in that quiescent morning hour, alone in that bungalow in the mountains, I did have it in my subconscious to relax and vacate the mortal husk. In that moment I knew that I knew how to do it. Deciding that I did want more of the same exquisite experience, I lay back on my pillow and opened the marvelous vault of the subconscious storehouse.

This time I deliberately felt myself quitting my body!

I felt the same blissful release, the same exquisite languor that precedes all forms of subconscious trance. I floated. I fell.

But this time no one "caught" me. *I seemed to walk out into the blessed white illumination of that exhilarating place.* Nor did it occur to me that even then I had done anything exceptionally wonderful. I went through the whole experience the second time as smoothly and unerringly as though I had fallen asleep and resumed a dream.

When I walked out into that Higher Reality the second time, however, a change had come over the portico itself.

It was filled with people!

They were coming into the structure from up the long corridor on the northern side. They sauntered into the room, and stood around regarding me, smiling at me quietly—as though they also knew a good joke about me—finally sauntering down the steps to the south in little groups of three's and four's. *Practically everybody nodded and spoke to me!* They had a kindness, a courtesy, a friendliness, in their faces and addresses that quite overwhelmed me. Think of all the saintly, attractive, magnetic folk you know, imagine them constituting the whole social world—no misfits, no tense countenances, no sour leers, no preoccupied brusqueness nor physical disfigurements—and the whole environment of life permeated with an ecstatic harmony as universal as air, and you get an idea of my reflections in those moments. I recall exclaiming to myself:

"How happy everybody seems! How jolly! Every person here conveys something that makes me want to know him personally."

Then with a sense of shock it dawned upon me:

"I have known every one of these persons at some time or other, personally, intimately! But they're sublimated now—physically glorified—not as I knew them in worldly life at all!"

I CANNOT make anyone understand how natural it all seemed that I should be there, particularly with them. After that first presentiment of dying, which experience had ended in the most kindly ministration as I have reported, all terror and strangeness left me and I never felt more alive. It never occurred to me on either occasion that I was in "heaven" or if it did, it occasioned me no more astonishment than that at some time in my adolescent consciousness it had occurred to me that I was on "earth." After all, do we know much more about one place than the other?

I had simply ended two queer voyages through bluish void and found myself each time in the same charming place among affable, worthwhile people who saw in me something that amused them to the point of quiet merriment. Yet not a merriment that I could resent.

I had no mad obsession to go off in search of Diety or look up Abraham Lincoln or Julius Caesar. I was quite content to stroll timidly in the portico by which I had entered this harmonious dimension and be greeted with pleasant nods by persons whose individualities were uncannily familiar.

They were conventionally garbed, these people, both men and women. I recall quite plainly that some of the women wore hats. The big, broad-shouldered, blue-eyed friend in white who had first received me with his hand beneath my neck, always hovered in my vicinity, I recall, and kept an eye on my whereabouts and conduct. . .

I PLEDGE my reputation on the solemn contention that I talked with these people, identified many of them—including two former Manhattan newspaper editors who had had much to do with launching me on the tempestuous seas of magazine authorship—called others by wrong names and was corrected, saw and did things that night that are *verboten* for me to narrate in a magazine article but which I recall with a minuteness of detail as graphic as I see the keys of my typewriter now under my fingers.

Regardless of the fact that imagination is the chief asset for one of my vocation—or what was my vocation up to that time—I am not given to particularly vivid dreams. Certainly we never dream by the process of coming awake first, knowing that we are suffering some abnormal kind of head or heart attack, swooning and coming abruptly conscious again in the arms of two kindly persons who reassure us audibly that everything is quite all right. Nor do the impressions of a dream stay with us—at least they have never stayed so with me—so that after months have passed such an experience is still as vivid as any of my experiences in Siberia during the late World War.

I went somewhere that night, penetrated to a distinct place and had an actual physical experience. I found myself an existing entity in a locality where those I had always called *"dead"* were not dead at all; they were alive with an alive-ness far transcending life in flesh.

The termination of this journey—my exit, so to speak—was as peculiar as my advent. I cannot print the true details, as they concern a person now living on earth. Furthermore, they would not be understood by the masses to whom this article may come, for as Jesus once said regarding the higher dimensions of life: If I tell you of earthly things and ye believe them not, how can ye believe when I tell you of heavenly things?

But to give you some idea of what I encountered, let me say this: In that mortally discarnate state myself, *I encountered the soul of a living person that had become released by normal sleep and was wandering in that Land of the Leal without knowing that it was there!* It would awaken on the morrow totally unaware of what it had done during the night. And greeting it as I did, in the form that I did, showing me its true character nakedly, so horrified and shocked me that I ran from it. As I ran, it followed blindly, not unlike a nightmare, *a creature with no eyes!*

I understand now what it was I saw, and why I saw it. I had called it to me by a subconscious process too complicated to enter into here. But running from it, I stumbled and fell as it was almost upon me in nightmare obsession.

Instantly, instead of real biliousness, I was caught in the swirl of bluish vapor again that seemed to roll in from nowhere in particular. Instead of plunging prone, I was lifted and levitated. Up, up, up, I seemed to tumble away from the ghastly apparition *feet first,* despite the ludicrousness of the description. A long, swift, swirling journey of this, as before. Then came that suffocating suffusion of greasy, cloying, sickish substance ending once more with the agonizing *click.* The best analogy is the sound my repeating deer-rifle makes when I work the ejector mechanism—a flat, metallic, automatic sensation.

Next, I was sitting up in bed in my physical body again, as wide awake as I am at this moment, staring at the patches of windows where the new day was coming brighter over the eastern mountains. But the same reflection of physical exhaustion was again through my diaphragm and abdomen, and it lasted several minutes. Not any digestive distress.

Simply a great weariness in my torso as though I had just passed through a great physical ordeal and my heart must accelerate to make up the lost energy.

"Those weren't dreams!" I cried aloud, half expecting to hear William's voice in rebuttal once more. But it did not come. Instead, Laska uncoiled from the foot of the bed and straightened to her haunches.

I looked at the clock on the table near at hand. The time was twenty minutes to five o'clock!

There was no more slumber for me that night. I lay back finally with the twin experiences fresh in my senses but with an awful lamentation in my heart that I was forced to come back at all—back into a world of struggle and disappointment, turmoil and misrepresentation, to an existence of bill collectors, unfriendly bankers, capricious editors and caustic critics—to all the mental and physical aches and pains which combine with the slings and arrows of outrageous fortune to make of this earth-plane a Vale of Tears.

It was tragedy, the Coming Back!

Particularly I dwelt on the one I had seen wandering in sleep, called to me by an act of my own. Not till weeks and months later was I instructed in exactly what had taken place that night, producing the latter phenomenon. But it was a common process, I learned. Thousands of us go out of our bodies and communicate with our "dead" on their own planes, while we are in the heaviest part of the night's cataleptic slumber. *But we do not bring the memory of it back into mortal consciousness.* Frequently, our adventures thus are the causes of our dreams. We are trying to picture to ourselves in terms of earth-form, what we have been through, and we have the vague dream distortions. Or we tell our relatives at the breakfast table: "I had a terribly vivid dream about Aunt Emily last night," Aunt Emily having departed this life weeks or months or years before. We actually *were* with Aunt Emily but in an entirely different plane of consciousness which we cannot recognize on that of the mortal.

Enough of that for the moment.

Call it the Hereafter, call it Heaven, call it Purgatory, call it any one of the Astral Planes, call it a Hyper-Dimension, call it What You Will. Whatever it is—and where—that human entities go after being released from physical limitations, I had gone there that night consciously, *and brought the full conscious memories of it back with me!* Like Lazarus of old, I had been called back, back to the anguish of physical existence to finish out my time and errand in the conventional manner.

For I did have an errand to finish out, and some day when the proper time has elapsed, and earthly event has proven the validity of my contention, I may reveal what I have had thus revealed to me, as to the specific details of that errand.

Up to the time of writing this article, almost a year later, I have not had the slightest inclination toward a repetition of the episode. Dreams I have had, and occasionally a fine old-fashioned nightmare, but have known them for such. Somehow or other, in sleep that night, with external aid or otherwise, I unhooked something in the strange mechanism that is Spirit in Matter and for two hours my own conscious entity that is Bill Pelley, writing-man, slipped over on the Other Side.

There is a survival of human entity after death of the body, for I have seen and talked intelligently with friends whom I have looked down upon as cold wax in caskets!

But that is not all. There is plenty of aftermath. To describe the details of the experience, however, it is necessary to intrude a few personal confidences, none of which I am eager to make.

I brought back something with me from that Ecstatic Interlude— something that had interpenetrated my physical self and which suddenly began to function in strange powers of perception!

AS I have said, I was born the only son of an itinerant Methodist minister. Soon after my birth my parents began that old-fashioned

Odyssey of traveling from "call" to "call" in the northern Massachusetts back hills.

Orthodox Protestant theology as it was forty years ago, was far more plentiful in my father's household than bread, butter, clothes and fuel, in those days. Camp meetings and Quarterly Conferences, the Higher Criticism, Predestination, Free Will and Election, Infant Damnation, hell fire and the Day of Judgment, constituted most of the household converse in my young and tender years. God early shaped up to me as a weird combination of heavenly Moloch and sublimated Overseer of the Poor.

Parish poverty forced my father from the ministry while I was in childhood but with grim New England rigor he saw to it that his relinquishment of a pulpit did not lessen my surfeit of conventional theology. Three times to church on the Sabbath day and twice during the week—Tuesday evening class meeting and Thursday night prayer meeting—left me small opportunity to forget my Creator in the days of my youth and the gratitude I owed Him. Just what this gratitude was owed Him *for*, troubled my small soul exceedingly in those far-off years because I found myself a perpetually hungry, shabbily-dressed, and none-too-happy youngster who had to start his life-labor at fifteen years of age and stay with it thereafter, even to the present.

Much Scripture was quoted to prove that my desire for a high school and college education was unfilial in view of the struggle father was having for survival. I ceased to be strong for Scripture after interest in my first mill-job had become a stalemate. I must further attest that the treadmill of a factory's discipline when other boys of my age were disporting themselves in healthy animal play, did not make me much stronger for God.

In the years between fifteen and twenty-two I became a smouldering little Bolshevik against every kind of authority, particularly against religious authority which had apparently sanctioned these injustices against me, and picking up the rudiments of a denied education by promiscuous reading, I went far afield from accredited Christianity.

No need to clutter up this article with the books I read, but at twenty-two, in a little town in northern New York State I was publishing a brochure magazine of heretical tendencies. Not exactly atheistic but holding few illusions about the Scriptures—as I knew them then—or about the Scribes and Pharisees who wail loudly in public places about their righteousness and who take good care that their alms are seen of men. I had discovered myself possessed of a certain facility with iconoclastic language, no censor, and the courage of my ignorance. Fresh from a wry, repressed childhood, cluttered up psychologically with the worst sort of New England inhibitions, revengeful that I had been denied social and academic advantages for which my hunger was instinctive, I proceeded to play a lone hand and make things hot for several goodly people whose only indictment was that they represented authority as aforesaid, especially spiritual authority. I know I made existence rather annoying for a number of representative ministers of the faith who saw life as through a glass darkly but weren't making the squall about it that I was making. From maturer perspective I quite affirm that I should have been spanked—or rather, educated—but all the theological misfits in forty-eight states and a couple of foreign countries were soon buying my magazine, unaware that it was being written by a beardless youth, and my twaddle and blither were piling up to give me much heartburn in later years when I came to see that I merely took out on God what I should have taken out on an inhibited environment.

The Almighty stood the onslaught rather well, however. I got into newspaper work as I have outlined, and into matrimony, and parenthood, and more poverty. And that was the last of the heretical magazine, though not of its owner's theological complexes. And eventually the day came when immature intelligence couldn't stand the pace and instead of digesting I ejected it *à la mal de mer* . . . for the next ten years I was practically an agnostic.

I had brains enough to see that my life had been started all wrong and was "getting no better fast," but not the academic equipment nor social balance to alter existence and start myself about-face.

Those were cruel, cruel years, looking back on them now. A couple of business projects went whack and after them my marriage. Family relatives made the whole mess worse by volunteering to "teach" me how to run my affairs. And my affairs—and life—had already been run too much by "teaching" relatives. With each additional snarl I got more and more vindictive. The death of my first daughter mellowed me somewhat. I wrote a couple of novels in which love of human nature was largely a reflex from the fearsome storm of hatred and despair that was waging inside me. I knew my life was a ghastly mess, that I was cynical and caustic, that the so-called "friends" I possessed, whom I could really trust, could be counted on the fingers of one hand— and most of them would stand watching at that—that we got nothing in this world unless we fought for it with all the ferocity of a Siberian wolf-dog and that beyond peradventure of a doubt, *death ended everything!*

America's entry into the world war found me in the Orient, as I have said, not a healthy place at all for one who was striving to escape the biological premise for human existence. I went with the Japanese forces to Siberia, acted as Red Triangle man, consular courier, and war correspondent through the Bolshevik-Czech campaign and came back to the United States to face a newspaper business in ruins. The swarming millions of Asia had not confirmed my faith in the conventional Almighty's goodness and wisdom, in fact they had only made me more skeptical than ever of His existence at all, *though I never had anything but a remorseful tenderness in my heart for the Man of Sorrows and what He epitomized in the scheme of things human.*

Curiously enough, however, this was strictly a personal relationship. It had nothing to do with my father's theology.

To save my newspaper creditors from loss, I went to Hollywood and labored among the flesh-pots. I made a score of motion pictures which rehabilitated my fortunes. I wrote an additional couple of novels that my publishers refused. I fought with them in consequence, still taking life by the strong-arm method. I wrote many stories that editors rejected. I fought with them also. When an editor wouldn't buy a story of mine that I considered particularly brilliant, I sat down at my typewriter and contrived to tell him that I thought him an ass. You see, I had the unfortunate complex that the attainment of success meant a knockdown and drag-out scrap. It made me a lone wolf at life, getting the least bit mangy as I reached my forties. . .

Time after time I tried sincerely to correct my psychology and get back certain religious—not theological—cues I felt that I had lost with the passing of boyhood. I plunged deeper than ever into eleven-pound volumes on all sorts of racial traits and behaviorisms. I was a walking museum of how a man may reach middle life and yet be the worst mess internally that ever got into *Who's Who in America but What of It?*

In view of such an autobiographical summary, the significance of the nocturnal experience in my mountain bungalow should not be abstruse.

I can look back now and recognize that throughout those forty years of turmoil and seeming unhappiness *I was being prepared for something.* It was all very deliberate. There was no chance in it anywhere. I had a definite work to do and those had been forty years of the most rigorous disciplining in order to acquire the experience to do that work efficiently. In no other environment, with no other parents, could I have gained all those spiritual things that I had truly been gaining without being aware of it. . .

Thousands, yes millions, of people are going through that same Golgotha today—not knowing they are acquiring invaluable experience and wisdom for a great work they definitely volunteered to do after getting into life. But they, like myself, must find the Key to the secret of that Golgotha in each case. It came to me in California in 1928 because without exactly knowing it, I had arrived at a balancing of the three factors in my being: the physical, mental, and spiritual. I was therefore ready to proceed with the larger employment.

THE FIRST intimation that I received, that the discarnate experience had affected me physically, was in going down into town next morning and into the office of one of my concerns. Soon I noted that the employees were conferring in little knots, whispering together, casting puzzled glances in my direction.

"Has anything especially happened to you?" one girl finally found courage to inquire.

"What makes you ask that?" I demanded, startled.

"Because somehow you don't seem the same person who went out of here two or three days ago. You've altered somehow. We can't make it out."

I went about my bungalow in the days that followed as though I were still in a sort of trance—which verily I was. Days of this, with a queer unrest galvanizing me, a feeling that I was on the verge of something, that out of my weird self-projection onto another plane of consciousness I had brought back something that was working in me like yeast.

Then came experience Number Two—not quite so theatric and therefore harder to describe.

One night while still imbued with the "feeling" of my fourth dimensional adventure, I decided to go to New York on a trip and consult with some friends there whom I knew to be interested in the Society for Psychical Research. I took down a volume of Emerson and tossed it into my bag for reading matter en route. The next day I was speeding eastward.

All day long I rode and the daylight died as we left the Golden State behind us. Off on the reaches of the Mojave Desert, the transcontinental train clicked along, mile on mile. The evening deepened. Passengers retired. I was finally left alone in the club car.

I had the volume of Emerson with me and had opened it to his *Over-Soul*. In the middle of it, though not reading any specific line, epigram, paragraph or page, I had a queer moment of confusion, a sort of cerebral vertigo. *Then a strange physical sensation played at the top of my head as though a great shaft of pure white light had poured down from above, boring straight through the roof of that droning Pullman coach and into my skull!*

In that instant a vast weight went out of my whole physical ensemble, a weight that had been forty years in concreting. A veil was torn away.

I was conscious of a Presence, a stupendous Presence. Something had happened and was continuing to happen. A cascade of pure, cool, wonderful *peace* was falling down from somewhere and completely cleansing me from every snarl and complex.

I knew in those moments that Jesus the Christ was an actual Personage!

I knew more.

I knew that He had been waiting forty years for me to come up through my curriculum of earthly experiencing, to arrive at that moment.

I knew that the churches, the theologians, the religionists, were all wrong about Jesus the Christ and that along with millions of others being blindly led and fed on arid allegorical interpretations of Truth, they were misrepresenting the Man of Galilee.

Jesus the Christ, and all that He meant to the world, *WAS!*

And again there was nothing maudlin about it, nothing sanctimonius, *nothing that had to do with religion.*

It was more than ever a personal relationship.

My book fell from my fingers to the car-carpet and stayed there. I sat staring into space. *I was not the same man I had been a few moments before!*

I mean this physically, mentally, spiritually. I knew that somehow I had acquired senses and perception that I could never hope to describe to any second person and yet they were as real to me as the shape of my hands. For a time I wondered if "much learning had driven me mad" but then I recalled that really mad people never stop to question whether or not they are balanced. Next I was aware of something new and strange in my whole experience—

I was conscious of presences about me, conversing. That empty Pullman held passengers not perceptible to mortal eye. And in a manner of speaking, *I could discern their thought-speech!*

I cannot tell in this article the contacts and adventures I confronted in New York, corroborating these presentiments. But I came back to my mountain bungalow a month later with these psychical gifts developed to a point where I knew full well the meaning of those strange manifestations in the house at which my dog had been so nervous.

From the very first night of my return I knew that there was someone in that darkening room with me beside Laska, my dog. In fact, I was aware that several living, vibrant personalities were with me in that room. Laska sat up, cocked her head from side to side and wagged her tail at some of them again—at *nothing* apparently—one of them in particular standing by my desk at the north end of the room. And now I understood!

And yet I was not in the slightest afraid. Why be afraid of our friends? . . .

In all of my life up to that time I had never seen a ghost, never had more than an academic interest in psychical phenomena, and pooh-poohed spiritualism as a sort of crack-brained dogma that belonged in the same pigeon-hole with soothsaying and gypsy fortune-telling. I had not invited any of these experiences that I knew of. They had simply *come to me.*

What really had happened was, I had unlocked hidden powers within myself that I know every human being possesses, and had augmented my five physical senses with other senses just as bonafide, legitimate, and natural as touch, taste, smell, sight, or hearing!

That I had help in unlocking these hidden powers I will not deny. Nevertheless, nothing had happened to me that has not happened to thousands of other people, only in very rare cases do they talk about it. What those hidden powers are, and why I maintain that they are bonafide, I will have to leave to other writings.

But they had suddenly shown me that life was not at all the ordinary, humdrum, three-meals-a-day thing that I had always accepted. Its essence and its meaning was so vast and fine and high and beautiful that it overwhelmed me and a recognition of it performed a sort of re-creation in me that made me feel I was not the same person I had been up till then.

My desire to explain intelligibly just what I mean by this, is almost an ache within me at this moment. But for some uncanny reason, words are not the medium that conveys it. The only term I can employ that comes anywhere near the truth is *spirituality*. The *me* that is the Bill Pelley entity can convey it by *being*, and the fact that I *am*, gets it to you.

Is this last a nonsensical statement? All I can say is, that I know by experience that there is a great overpowering existence outside of what we call worldly Life—that I have been in it and felt it—that having been in it has endowed me with certain capacities that have transformed my whole concept of the universe and some of my friends are kind enough to add, have transformed *me*. Physically as well as mentally.

My first dramatic physical reaction was a sudden change in the physical components of my body. I discovered that miraculously I had lost my "nerves." . . .

Ever since childhood I had lived under such a tremendous nervous tension that it had kept me underweight, put lines on my face and an edge on my voice, shattered me psychologically so that opposition of any kind infuriated me and made me want to crash through it like an army tank flattening out a breastworks. Attacks of indigestion were so common that I no longer gave them thought. The tobacco I consumed had its basis in the gnawing desire to anesthetize this nervousness.

Suddenly this had departed.

I was peaceful inside.

I had the glorious feeling of physical detachment from the handicaps of bodily matter. No form of bodily exertion seemed to take energy that I need consciously supply. I had always been slightly stoop-shouldered. Without any unusual exercise my spine straightened of itself, so to speak, and my shoulders felt broadened.

Along with this physical alteration went the unexplainable faculty to withstand fatigue either active or sedentary. If I wearied myself by tremendous labor, it was the healthy weariness of boyhood that overtook me. On the other hand, I could sit at my typewriter twelve hours at a stretch if necessary with scarcely a muscle protesting such inactivity.

With this alteration came a different feeling toward those around me. I discovered that I couldn't fight with people any more, and that I was making friends. A queer statement, this. Yet people were going out of their way to perform services for me, to counsel me, to seek my society, to make me one with themselves. I think this amazed me more than the strangeness of my new physical rebirth.

And yet deep down underneath it all . . well, I understood. That understanding, I aver, has been growing with me every day and hour since, comprising naturally many things that I am restrained from offering in a magazine that is read by all classes of people at all stages of mental, moral, and spiritual development. Still, there are conclusions and equations I may draw that have universal application.

WHAT is this thing that happened to me, and why did it happen?

First, I believe my subconscious hunger after what the Bible terms "the things of the spirit"—that is, the sincere desire to penetrate behind the mediocrity of three-meal-a-day living and ascertain what mystery lay behind this Golgotha of Existence—had what might be called a "prenatal basis." It had to do with my coming into life in the first place. Vaguely, dimly, all through my life up to that memorable night in California, I had remembered something that I was supposed to do, to accomplish, in life, and the fact that I was not accomplishing it—that I could recognize with any inward satisfaction—was taking me out of my character and making me the infuriated young wretch that resented authority the clock around. The fact that I had responded at last to the Higher Call, that morning in Beverly Hills, turned my life around abruptly even as I had turned my car around literally, attracted to me spiritual forces of a very high and altruistic order who aided me in making that hyperdimensional visitation.

Second, it goes without saying that having made such a visitation and having had certain questions concretely answered by those I confronted in that dimension, my subconscious—or for that matter conscious—knowledge of what the Fourth Dimension is, and means, and what can be done within its area, undertook to operate first upon my physical body and performed the rejuvenation that subsequently came to me. And yet I can no more explain the Fourth Dimension with *words* than I can convey to a man blind from birth what I mean when I talk about the *redness* of the color Red. I know what the higher dimension is, myself, as I know what redness is by having eyes. I can see how it interpenetrates Matter, constituting the "inside" of it, so to speak, and how projections from it must come out the reverse of what we know them on the physical plane. But I can no more make it intelligible to the average reader than Einstein can explain Relativity to a group of salesmen in a smoking car. The average man or woman without his spiritual perceptions duly awakened, cannot possess any equipment to assimilate what I am trying to tell him—anymore than the blind man can assimilate the "redness" of red if he never had eyes capable of knowing the peculiar attributes of Light in Matter that give the phenomenon of color, or any more than expounders of Relativity can convey their meanings to those unfamiliar with higher mathematics.

Third, these experiences—the visitation, the knowledge that was bestowed in the visitation and the result of it—immediately revealed to me that there is a world of subliminal existence interpenetrating the ordinary world in which most of us exist as average two-legged Americans full of aches and worries, *and that this subliminal world is the real world*—the world of "stern reality" if you will—that is waiting for the race to learn of it and tap its beneficent resources long before what we call physical death, that our "dead" loved ones are existent in it, alive and happy, conscious of their condition and waiting for us to join them either at "death" or at any time that we attain to that stage of spirituality where it is fitting for them to make contact *and remember it!*

Understand thoroughly, I am not a spiritualist, a Mystic, or a Psychic Researcher in the ordinary meaning of those terms. I am not trying to convert anyone to anything. I am simply telling you that something happened to me that was not consciously self-invited, that my friends attest to an even greater alteration having occurred in my personality than I am capable of feeling from within, although I feel plenty.

Having had certified that there is no such thing as Death for the conscious and sentient entity that is You and Me as we know one another, I find this certainty the touchstone that unlocks many another

38

mystery. What I have learned about the Life Fundamentals, that night and since, explains why one man is born rich and another poor, one a splendid athlete and another a helpless cripple, explains the friendships we make and the mates we marry, the poor luck or good fortune that accrues to us, why we put work and worry and love into the raising of children only to have them snatched from us at the threshold of maturity. It unlocks the mystery of the Christian religion as it was in its pristine purity, the miracles of Jesus, the conversional power of the Holy Spirit. It makes life strong and beautiful and true and fine—something to be lived without fear or doubt or unhappiness—and I think the experience happened to me *because it is my earthly brevet as time goes on to delineate in book and preachment something of the spiritual "redness of red"* if that conveys my meaning to those who may be interested.

There is in every human heart a hunger and a thirst for the things of the Spirit but in many of them this desire has become so embalmed with the poisons of worries, doubts, fleshly desires, struggles to attain the wherewithal for physical survival, that for all practical purposes it no longer exists.

The day is coming in the evolution of the race when Spirituality is going to be the whole essence of life instead of the present world's materialism. Here and there are those who because of their prenatal identities, so to speak, their consequent re-awakenings, their visions self-invited or otherwise, may be called monitors and mentors for their fellows, showing them what may be attained by anyone if he so orders his life and thinking as to be susceptible to such revelations.

I believe that Nature, God, Universal Spirit—give the Great Cause any name you will—is taking this method of giving the monitors and mentors unusual experiences to furnish the whole race an inspiration by which it may quicken its spiritual pace. There is nothing more prohibitive morally or ethically in exploring these great new fields of Reality than in exploring the fields of radio or atomic energy. In fact, *the Great Cause means we shall explore them!*

At any rate, whether I am right or wrong, I know that for a limited time one night in 1928, out in California, my spiritual entity left my physical body and went somewhere, a concrete place where I could talk, walk about, feel and see, and have answers returned to my questions addressed to physically "dead" people, that have checked up in the waking world and clarified for me the whole riddle of earthly existence.

I know there is no Death because in a manner of speaking I went through the process of dying, came back into my body, went out again deliberately, came back into it again and took up the burden of earthly living again. I know that the experience has metamorphosized the cantankerous Yankee that was once Bill Pelley and launched him into a wholly different universe that seems filled with much love, harmony, good humor and reasonable prosperity.

What's the answer to that?

There is no answer, except that it must be accepted as inevitably as I am forced to accept the awareness of my own identity.

I *know* because I have *experienced.*

And further deponent sayeth not.

II

THREE YEARS have now elapsed since I wrote the foregoing article for *The American Magazine*. I believe I have now had time to digest the significance of my hyperdimensional experience and see the episode in its proper perspective.

At first I was dubious about writing the article. It was a very deep personal experience and its nature was such that I did not care to have myself labeled a freak or a crank. But *The American Magazine's* editors persuaded me, and so the story was written and published.

I decided suddenly to accede to their request. When I brought in the manuscript, the March number of the magazine for 1929 had already gone to press. They halted the presses, had the forms taken off, and the first article removed and held over, to give space to *My Seven Minutes in Eternity*. Which meant that my manuscript had to be cut and shortened to fit exactly the space thus rendered available, even to the line and the word. So long as this enforced condensation did not militate against either the facts or the purport of the message, I could offer no objection. The only regrettable feature was that I had no opportunity in the space thus at my disposal to delineate the *two* passings out of my body in the one night, or explain that the title was largely derived from my friend William's suggestion, "Now don't try to see everything in the first *seven minutes!*" Many people were consequently under the impression that my experience lasted only seven minutes and they wonder honestly how I could have crammed so much into such an incredibly short span of time.

The circulation of *The American Magazine* in 1929 was around 2,250,000 copies. National advertisers estimate that each copy of a given magazine is read by at least four persons. Which means that something like *ten million people* had access to that narrative in its original form as published, and because it was the first article in the magazine for the month, most of them read it.

I know because of my mail in reaction.

I have told in my series of published papers written since, *"Why I Believe the Dead are Alive!"* the exactly detailed denouement following my epochal adventure, entering into the finest phases of my experiences since in what seems to be tantamount to a volume of Psychic Memoirs. Sufficient to say here that immediately the *American* article was published, things commenced happening in the offices of the magazine. Mail addressed to the editor, or to me as author of the narrative, assumed proportions analogous to that of Col. Charles Lindbergh after his epochal flight to Paris. I happened to be back in California at the time. Frantic trans-continental telephone calls began to reach me from New York imploring me to return and take up the task of answering the great mass of correspondents who wanted more light on my extraordinary experience.

I returned to New York and began the long labor of sorting, classifying, analyzing, and answering this plethora of letters. *It took me from six to nine months, with the aid of two secretaries.* The stranger part is, those letters are still arriving—because of a magazine article published three years ago—and my replies still keep one typist busy the better part of each day.

These letters in reaction, I discovered, grouped themselves into three divisions: The great mass came from persons *who declared they had undergone a similar experience* at some time in their lives and wanted to compliment me on telling mine publically; the next largest assortment came from those who were neither facetious, skeptical, nor derogatory, but who merely wanted more light on my sensations or the details of the environment in which I found myself; in the third class was that great army of spiritually minded people who only wanted to thank me for giving them an incentive toward stronger Christian faith and to implore me not to rest content with the writing of one article.

And here is an astounding fact: *Out of all the mail that resulted from the publication of "Seven Minutes in Eternity" less than 24 actual communications derided me as an eccentric, or expressed open disbelief that I was sane or telling the truth!*

The great army of English-speaking people who read of my experience paid me the compliment of taking my account at its face value and asked only that I answer specific questions about that Fourth Dimension in which I testified that those they loved but had temporarily lost, were dwelling.

NOW CONSIDERING the reactions from the experience, both upon my readers and upon myself and consequent fortunes, there is much to be said. Let me discuss the prodigious reader-reaction first.

The most gratifying surprise that I encountered was of course the discovery that I had not been peculiar in my adventure: that hundreds upon hundreds of quite normal persons from time to time throughout their lives had left their physical bodies under different provocations and visited the same higher levels of consciousness which I had explored so dramatically that night. But most of them had lacked the courage even to tell relatives, fearing an arraignment for falsehood or insanity.

I know that the vast majority of these persons *were* telling me the truth because in their letters they went to considerable length to acquaint me with details, particulars, and items of *their* experiences which were substantially identical with details I had undergone but *not* mentioned in my public magazine account, and some of which I had not even mentioned to my closest friends.

I submit that two or more people, unknown to one another, who had traveled to Japan for instance, could easily tell on meeting in later years whether the others had really been to the Land of the Cherry Blossoms by a comparison of what they saw and experienced in that altogether-charming country. It was so with me and my correspondents. In some cases they reminded me of details that had actually slipped my memory.

And here is a still more interesting check-up: In 95 per cent of these testimony letters, the technique of getting into the Higher Dimensions and the scenes and experiences encountered there, were so similar as to almost postulate a Law of the Process. A man in Oregon and a woman in Virginia would write me of similar visitations made by them, both recounting accurate details and specifications which I had not mentioned, and neither knowing of the other's letter.

In most of these instances, the visitation came as mine came: unheralded and unexpected. Neither did it come always in the aftermath of sickness, drug addiction, or time of great trouble. But invariably it *did* come in the wake of a tremendous desire for spiritual truth and a hunger and thirst after things of the spirit. And let me add that the writers of the letters in this class were not drawn from among any one type of person, any one sect, cult, age, occupation, social stratum, or locality of residence.

The letters people wrote me came from a clean-cut cross-section of Americans, from railroad and bank presidents, from stenographers and street-car conductors, of every age in years from octogenarians to boys and girls in college, men and women being represented equally.

And another startling fact was: that if any one class of inquirers was particularly noticeable in this mass, it was composed of Protestant ministers, most eager of all to lead their flocks into a clearer understanding of the eternal verities.

Here again, my eyes were opened. This was not like the theology of the old days. Was something coming over humanity, a general awakening, of which my own experience had merely been precursor?

The article, I might say, was copied in innumerable religious journals, and during the first year my own staff, or that of *The American Magazine,* learned of 144 sermons preached by clergymen on the experience in question.

In only one instance was a skeptical attitude taken by a pastor. This exception came from a minister in California who sincerely believed the devil had tampered with my soul that night because I had not encountered Our Lord when I found myself on the Inner Side of Life's Veil. . . .

I found, I say, that such a discarnate visitation was common to vast numbers of people, but they took no trouble to convince others not so fortunate because of the facetiousness with which they had assumed they would be greeted.

Going out of the body, consciously or unconsciously, is a common experience among persons of all races, creeds, and strata of society! Only I had caused a sensation by describing it in the lead article of a periodical having ten million readers. And in view of the fact that the great majority of those who from time to time so enter other planes of being report similar sights and experiences, it is not difficult to accept the thesis that here is a field which society may well explore to its profit.

THE SECOND class of my correspondents universally wanted to know how much of the article was fact and how much fiction. Some of them would pick out tiny discrepancies of phraseology and context, of which any person writing at high speed in the exhilaration of composition might be guilty, and offer them as evidence that fabrication seemed evident in certain sequences of my narrative.

To this class of questioner I wrote a personal letter wherever practicable, assuring each one that whereas whole sequences of my narration were deleted in the interests of common credibility—because dogmatic church people might take umbrage at the magazine for printing such an article at all, *everything that did get printed was cold-blooded fact, to the best of my knowledge and memory!* There was no deliberate fiction in the article and it was not written to make a literary sale or enhance my reputation by sensationalism. The editors of *The American Magazine* will attest that I wrote the article under protest, that I abhorred having the indictment of "going Conan Doyle" attached to my name as a writing man. At the time that I was persuaded to do it,

46

none of us knew whether it would be accepted by the public or whether we would be charged with perpetrating a hoax. We realized that we were pioneers of a sort, and due to the fact that I could not go the whole way and tell everything, I was risking my reputation on one grand game of "pitch and toss" . . . happily the experiment came out all right insofar as *The American Magazine* was concerned. As for myself, it has only been within the past year that I have begun to see the experience in its true significance and realize what stupendous power was at work that night, altering my career deliberately for a most incredible reason. More of this later.

In this second class of correspondents, wanting more light on phenomena so amazing as those I had professed to set forth, I grouped also those learned psychologists, psychiatrists, and physiologists, who went to the trouble of composing monographs to convince the editors of *The American Magazine* that they must have lent themselves to a hoax, in that what had happened to me was much the same sort of hallucination which they treated daily. Others offered lengthy argument that I must certainly be a secret user of drugs, or that the experience resulted from the prodigious use of tobacco.

What I could not tell these eminent professors was the same thing that I could not delineate to the magazine's other readers, and which I have not told to many persons outside of a circle of intimate friends. It was a thing that could be told only to those who had witnessed the results of the phenomena in my life and affairs since: *the persistence of the strange supersensitive powers which were awakened in me by contact with those on the Other Side that night, and how that contact has been preserved in uninterrupted sequence ever since.*

LET THE modern psychologists and psychiatrists explain these "hallucinations" as they will, I submit that hallucinations do not endow us with supernormal perceptions, that they do not enable us to contact so-called dead people exactly as though they were alive.

My "mental radio" was awakened by my experience to such an extent that I can tune in on the minds and voices of those in another dimension of Reality. I can carry on conversations with them for myself or for others without trance of any kind, proffer questions and get sensible, intelligent, and ofttimes invaluable answers.

And that brings me to the second great evaluation of my experience and a hint of the true significance of what occurred to me that night in its bearing on my career and on current religious thought.

I have said that my life seemed at sixes and sevens up to the moment when I turned my car back from that blind road at the south side of Beverly Hills. I had let myself grow up a nervous, cantankerous, disgruntled person, blaming my parents for what I had missed, blaming God for not shedding more illumination on a dark human pathway. But there was a deeper reason for my disgruntlement than I have generally spoken or written about.

From the day that I left school, up to the morning of that motor trip to Beverly Hills, I had felt that I was a misfit in life.

I couldn't find my true niche, and knew it!

Despite the fact that I was one of the best-paid short-story writers in America, that from time to time I had made sums from my novels sufficient to keep me the rest of my life, that my success in the movie field was the envy of a great group of fellow-writers, *I had known for fifteen years that writing was not my forte.*

I puzzled and ofttimes nettled Manhattan magazine editors when I would not settle down and work steadily at my vocation, despite the demand that existed for my work. There is one fiction editor in New York who took me severely to task time and time again, because of my caustic and derisive attitude toward so-called current literature as a vocation for a healthy, active man. Again and again this editor argued patiently, calling my attention to the good my stories had done people by their own comment sent the magazine.

"Sitting down at a typewriter and pounding out words all day is a fine job for a full-grown man!" I decried.

"What do you think you want to do? What is a real job?" this editor would query me.

I would shrug my shoulders. I was inarticulate at something deep inside me that would not form itself in words. "All I know is," I would lament, "this isn't my job. It's bigger than this. It has to do with vast masses of people, scattered all over the earth. It isn't political and yet it seems to have something to do with foreign nations. It has something to do with publishing on a colossal scale. It has something to do with great hospital ships, with the direction of some great philanthropic enterprise. Beside it, this work of grinding out entertaining stories is puerile and silly."

Again and again I registered the vague details of this larger work, *as far back in my life as* 1907. I confided it to New York friends in 1923. My particular editor friend would look at me sadly.

"You're like the successful comedian who insists on playing Hamlet!" I would be told. "You've got a market for a particular line of fiction for which some writers would give their eye-teeth, and you're contemptuous of it, and will only fill it as you're forced by economic pressure to earn money. You ought to be ashamed of yourself!"

I was doubly miserable in those times. How could I express something that seemed just under the threshold of consciousness but which would never quite come up where I could recognize it for what it was?

I BROKE away from New York in 1923, almost scuttling a publishing business that I had embarked upon there briefly in my efforts to find The Thing that Plagued Me. I went to California wondering if it awaited me there. Truth to tell, my disgruntlement at life was as much due to this weird inward pressure, this presentiment of a role I had to fill that I could not connect with, as at my environment or my early background.

What on earth ailed me? Why did I feel stifled? Why did I embark on business venture after business venture, only to see it fritter out, or to leave it half-way toward the success it really merited?

I know now that I was carrying in my subconscious mind a one-hundred per cent consciousness of my life's brevet and was anxious to be at it, not knowing that factors of Time and Situation—not to mention self-development and self-balance—had to be complied with, first!

When I turned my back on all that I had let myself become up to the present, that morning in Beverly Hills, and went hunting that bungalow in Pasadena, I was truly "remembering forward" certain things I had to do to put myself deliberately on the main track of my career. The months I spent in that bungalow before the Main Experience came that started the brevet up out of subconsciousness, were only an interlude of quiet and repose preparing me for the true revelation.

I could not write this in *The American Magazine* at the time, as part of my article. People wouldn't have understood. I could not have written it at any time before the present moment.

But this thing happened—just as it may well happen to hundreds of others in a similar predicament—*with the awakening of my psychical faculties as a result of the experience, the whole program of my life came clear!*

Call it that I had made a sort of Pact to come into mortal life, accomplish a certain work and attain a given objective. All that had gone before had been mortal, or physical, preparation for that Job. Of course I had not been able to perceive it while knocking through experience after experience. But at last I was no longer inarticulate about my life.

I had certain things to do and stood now on the threshold of concrete accomplishment!

IT BEGAN to come to me "psychically" soon after my return from my first New York trip.

I first discovered that if I relaxed myself, and put myself in a poised, acquiescent mood, *someone would come and talk to me!*

The Voice seemed like "fresh language drifting across the mind." A sense of joy and exhilaration was felt. And when I got pencil and paper and recorded, or dictated, the "instruction" I found that I had taken down intelligence that by no stretch of my own imagination could I possibly have composed, subconsciously or otherwise.

Again I refer those who want the literal story of what I went through in those first six or eight months, perfecting myself in this gift of Clairaudience, to my monograph of papers *"Why I Believe the Dead Are Alive!"* But night after night, month after month, I was taking down amazing documents of the most profound erudition: papers on theological origins, papers on cosmic physics, on atomic energy, on racial histories of peoples who had totally passed from the annals of men's knowledge.

Where was this material coming from? *I had read no such books. I had heard no one lecture on these subjects.* I had found I was getting material that in some cases augmented the most profound modern sciences. Certainly I was getting answers to hundreds of abstruse questions propounded to me by those who wrote me about *Seven Minutes in Eternity.*

The matter mounted up, five hundred pages, a thousand, *two thousand!*

What was I to do with it?

One night in the summer of 1929, the same Voice that had addressed me in my California bungalow, directing me "to relax and come back . . because you know well in your subconscious mind how to do it" announced that with the forthcoming week I should commence the transcript of a lengthy book that would be dictated to me and which when printed would go far toward clarifying for my correspondents innumerable questions they had asked.

I proceeded to take this book.

It came over in the form of a fictional presentation.

It was *Golden Rubbish!*

Geo. P. Putnam's Sons published *Golden Rubbish* in the fall of that year. This is not the place to give the history of that book or the strange reception it met with as contrasted with *Seven Minutes in Eternity*. Sufficient to say here that it was the fictional exposition of a young woman whose life had paralleled my own up to that date, and whose awakening to the eternal verities conveyed many things that could not be put in a personal article.

Regardless of the testimony I have since received that *Golden Rubbish* has helped hundreds of persons greet the Great Beyond with poise and peace, the book was scarcely heard from. Putnam's published one edition and then abruptly discontinued it from their list.

But long before *Golden Rubbish* was in type I was at work on a second volume that was giving me no little concern.

This second book was emphatically not fiction, and it has never seen type; it still lies in manuscript locked away in my files. It consisted of about 400 pages of directly prophetic material, forecasting the events of the world in the next dozen years.

Now at last I began to perceive, in a sort of fearsome stupefaction, the true cause of my inward urges, my business fiascoes, my temperamental disgruntlements at life, before May, 1928.

I was having my part and role in these events prognosticated for me! For the first time in thirty to forty years I was learning facts about myself and future that "clicked" with something inside me that had always been too deep for utterance.

THIS BOOK, with a mass of supporting discourses, began a great castigation of the false religious concepts and systems that had entangled human life and spiritual thinking, and lined the peaceful precepts of the Christ behind great national armaments, making for wars and rumors of wars.

It said that a complete and utter alteration of society was on the make, to be ushered in with a great collapse on the bourses of the world in the coming autumn. Bear in mind that I was getting this in the summer of 1929 when the country was at the height of its speculative prosperity.

I was told of secret events transpiring abroad, of the machinations of great international financiers and statesmen, whose movements were being carefully watched by unseen witnesses, whose plans and conspiracies were known, who would not only bring about a prolonged financial depression but who would make a concerted attempt in time to overthrow constructive world governments.

It was fully delineated in this book that a great contest was in prospect. All the dark, malignant forces in the cosmos were lining up for a great trial of strength with the white constructive Christ Forces, and the contest would be cataclysmic. Humanity was to be sharply divided into two great classes: those who were *for* the Christ and all His works, and those who hated Him and would try to defeat His people in flesh and put them in a sort of vassalage.

Page after page, chapter after chapter, much of it too incredible to believe at that time, with the interval for performance so short.

Then began to come out the true significance of *Seven Minutes in Eternity.*

"You were given that experience," my unseen but plainly heard monitors went on, "to acquaint you with the fact that you came into mortal life some two-score years ago, to assist in this contest on the worldly side. You belong to a Union of Spiritual Mentors and Counsellors in the Higher Realms of Life whose mission it is to guide humanity in times of this stress. You went into an earthly body at a time that would allow you to go through the experiences of adolescence and reach balanced maturity as the Crisis neared. All of the experiences you underwent as a lad were by foreordainment, to equip you mentally and spiritually for the part that you and others must play in the ushering in of this New Order among men. It was part of the Plan that you were to be kept in ignorance of this role until the years had arrived for you to function. That time is now at hand.

"You will find that during the next two years, through no agencies within your control, you will be at the head of a great spiritual movement, not only national but international as well.

You will be guided along strange avenues and into strange offices. *Be surprised at nothing!* There are hundreds of your brethren also in life with you. They do not all know their identities and roles, anymore than you have known yours. But they will make themselves known to you. There will be no mistaking them. Together you will perform a goodly service to the present human race and guide it out of its forthcoming quandaries under the Greater Leadership of Jesus the Christ."

There was more, much more. But this was its tenor.

I submit that this sort of thing coming suddenly over the Cosmic wire disconcerted me badly. I said little or nothing to my friends about it, fearing an indictment for possessing an energetic superiority complex. If I were getting accurate material from a trustworthy source, future events would show in proof. I would simply wait and see.

In November the stock markets cracked, exactly as had been foretold. Russia announced her Five-Year-Plan, exactly as had been foretold. The great Atheistic Movement got under way, exactly as had been foretold.

By the spring of the following year the Depression was upon the nation and the world in earnest. Day after day I picked up my morning paper to find headlines that tallied to a hair with prophecies that had been given me privately months before.

I had to accept the designation and labors allotted to me, *against my will!* But just how I was to cut into the international scrap, just how I was going to be inducted into all this world turmoil, a mere writer of fiction in a New York apartment, was wholly beyond me. How I was to head a nation-wide spiritual revival in less than 20 months should have given any sane person cause for abandoning the whole business as delusions of grandeur.

And yet the messages kept coming, more and more significant of import. Information was being put into my hands that would have been priceless to great financiers or captains of industry, could they have realized how authentic and dependable it was. And I could do nothing with it except to lock it away in files.

By May the responsibility of this material, plus the increasing correspondence that was pouring in to me from all quarters of the nation as a result of my continued psychic writings, persuaded me that I should at least make some gesture to begin to get this intelligence out to others.

Then again, people were sending me *their* psychical predictions, which they were receiving night on night from *their* mentors, and asking my opinion upon them. How could I tell them that they tallied with mine to a hair? Something certainly was "on the make" when such mysterious agencies were at work so accurately to warn certain persons throughout humanity of what impended, and what they were supposed to do to alleviate physical, mental, and spiritual distress.

I had repeatedly been told throughout these months of transcript, what some of my own previous earth lives had been, when I had done exactly this sort of labor before—and successfully. Still, I could not accredit it because I had little in my conscious mind that corroborated such declarations. The hard-headed New England training I had received in business and newspaper work, would not let me float around in clouds of grandiose delusions. Thank God for that!

And yet I was worried. Supposing there were much that I should be doing?

Supposing that all I was receiving was the truest part of truth?

The article in *The American Magazine* had long since sunk to insignificance beside the overwhelming flood of psychical material that was "coming over," directing me specifically in my affairs and relationships, almost without a slip or falter. Much as it meant to spiritually distraught persons about America to have the attestment of a man in my position, the real crux of the incident was indeed its aftermath.

Lest the skeptical doubt the origin of such material, and contend that it had bubbled up from my subconscious, let me relate this brief anecdote:

After one of my discourses one evening with a Great Brain not now operating in a physical vehicle, I heard another voice speaking in a language I did not understand. I asked the stenographer at my elbow to write out phonetically in long-hand the words of this strange language as I heard and repeated them. Word by word she took them down, marking the vowel signs properly so that later we might read them phonetically.

Twelve pages of this strange script were recorded. Several weeks later I showed them to an erudite philologist *who found over a thousand words of pure Sanskrit composing a sensible message that had to do with the present-day happenings in world affairs already spoken to me in English!* This was not wholly the modern Sanskrit now used in some parts of India. It purported to come from an ancient Atlantean soul who declared he had not incarnated in the mortal form for a period of 65,000 years. . . This message was given me in that ancient language presumably to refute those superficial scholars who delight to explain one of Nature's most significant manifestations by naming it all the "workings of the Subconscious" . .

And this Atlantean message bore out in detail the events still in the future for America and for the world. One night I exclaimed with some stress:

"Just what is it that you on the Other Side of life are trying to accomplish on this side through instruments like myself? Can you give me a brief but trenchant agenda of exactly your goal and purpose?"

Immediately this reply was dictated, swifter than it takes me to copy it in this narrative:

"We are presenting through you and your fellows of Our Order the complete delineation of a New World Society, politically, sociologically, and religiously, building by a new terminology what is the essence of that new society, not conceived by a few men after their own whims but as conceived by those who are planning the new world state from the Higher Dimensions of Time and Space. . .

"It encompasses a new World Program, beginning with the standards upon which religious thinking is based as being the starting point for the application of a new set of ethical and sociological principles, both practical and academic. . .

"This grand work has not been conceived in a day but is the outgrowth of a union of master-minds who have been many ages conceiving and discarding from the fruits of both experience and observation what is both wanted and needed in an entirely new social order. . .

"This concept is two-fold in principle, making man to understand his destiny *here* and making man to understand his destiny *hereafter*— or to put it in another way, on both sides of the Veil called physical death, for essentially there is but one life having these two phases. . ."

I WAS no longer skeptical as the spring of 1930 wore on, that something should be done. So many corroborations were coming in that what I had received was bonafide and accurate, so many people were appearing strangely in my affairs, that I could no longer ignore that I must indeed have a vital job to do, and the sooner I tried it out, the better for all concerned, myself especially.

I must ignore the criticisms of little souls that knew nothing of the gale in the wind and lamented that a passable fiction writer had been ruined to make a questionable metaphysician. I must push my New England practicality into the background for a time, till I learned whether or not I was being definitely called to that which my increasing messages implied.

My first experiment was to plan out some sort of periodical that should be the means for feeling my way into whatever larger work was awaiting ahead. I had long debated doing this, for my plethora of mail was requiring detailed answers to questions and problems of a spiritual nature that I could by no means answer in detail. I had found that my monthly grist of letters, regardless of the fact that the publishing of

Seven Minutes lay months in the background, grouped themselves into categories. Large numbers of correspondents all wanted answers to practically the same queries. What better way to reply to them than to take each one of these categories, write my answers in the form of lengthy magazine articles and then send my correspondents the magazine containing such articles? I had been for twenty years a publisher. I knew the magazine field "inside out and through the middle."

So in May, 1930, I brought out the first issue of *The New Liberator.*

SOME people have said that I chose the title unwisely; that it savored of a radical periodical and might be misinterpreted by the very masses I wanted to reach.

But I was getting my instructions and knew what was being worked out and why. I started a 48-page popular monthly, in which I printed from issue to issue the most significant psychical expositions I had received, answering the greatest number of letters from people who asked for such information specifically.

The acclaim that greeted *The New Liberator* was instantaneous. It began to connect me with persons about the nation whom I recognized as being part of the Goodly Company implied in my psychic admonitions. But it had not been running long, when another development of far greater significance took place.

Certain advanced souls, reading *The New Liberator* from month to month, gradually started writing me to the following effect:

"We are reading between the lines of the articles in the magazine that there is much which you are holding back. We can appreciate that this is feasible and astute. But there are a great group of us who consider ourselves sufficiently developed to stand strong meat in the way of advanced instruction and we are looking to you to advise us just what is ahead in worldly event. Is there not some way that you can duplicate this advanced material and get it out to us privately, even if only in mimeographed form?"

I received so many letters to this effect, from widely scattered sections of the country, and from people unknown to one another, that I finally decided I should act upon them.

The New Liberator had been running about a year when I sent out a general announcement to its subscribers that on the 3rd of May, 1931, I intended to prepare and mail to whomsoever applied to me, a special set of Cosmic Lessons that should contain material of a revelatory nature along the lines I had been getting for a year, *provided those who received those papers would get little groups of truth-seeking friends about them and read them the material on its arrival weekly!*

THE FIRST lesson was mailed out on May 3rd.

Again the repercussion was instantaneous. Thirty people applied for the first paper, which meant that thirty groups were getting the information all at the same time. The second week this number became fifty. The third week it was a hundred. The fourth week it was two hundred. By the beginning of the third month, in the hottest part of the summer of 1931, in the midst of increasing economic distress, the number was up in the neighborhood of *three hundred.*

And these were not "little groups of personal friends" seizing on this cosmic information and devouring it avidly week on week. The "instructors" whom I soon designated as Chaplains, were soon hiring halls and auditoriums to accommodate the crowd pushing in to hear the papers read. . . .

Again psychical prophecy was coming true! The messages had said that within less than 20 months I would be "at the head of a nation-wide spiritual movement having as its purpose the guidance of humanity throughout the troublesome times ahead." By September first I found myself sending out the weekly messages in printed form to thousands of people, and the staff to attend to all the detail of the "movement" had outgrown the staff of *The New Liberator Magazine.*

I had not wanted to start any new cult or sect. There were far too many in existence already—to baffle and confuse humanity. I had merely wanted to gather a goodly number of instructors throughout the nation and pass on to spiritually hungry and economically distressed people information of a supernal character apparently coming down from much higher and wiser planes of life.

So I systematized these instructors under the name of *The League of Liberators.*

AS I WRITE these words at the beginning of September, 1931, I am confronting an autumn in which *The League of the Liberators* may easily swell to a thousand audiences. Already there is talk in certain quarters of using these Great Master Scripts as the basis for the founding of *The Church of the Liberation.* I may not be able to stop this movement. It is getting beyond my control.

Personally I have other things of a more practical nature to occupy my time. It is a far cry back to that May night in 1928 when I went upstairs to bed debating the origin, nature, and reasons for races of men. I had reached a definite milestone in my earthly career. Before morning agencies were to be at work that were to start the uplift in my personal fortunes and functioning, to the present moment.

People thought when I published *My Seven Minutes in Eternity* in *The American Magazine* that it was merely the account of an epochal spiritual experience attesting to the fact of human survival. I cannot go along further without admitting that the publishing of *Seven Minutes* was merely the prelude to the colossal task that is on the way: bringing home to the masses the splendorful Illumination and Revelation that is to be made known to all men everywhere, of the completion of the work of The Christ in this our present generation.

For I have now seen too much transpire in worldly event, confirming all these psychic prognostications, to doubt my own obligation undertaken prenatally, if such a thing is conceivable. Humanity faces a terrific "plowing under" between the date of this present writing and September, 1936. Why I set that latter date specifically, I am not at this time allowed to divulge. But those who are readers of *The New Liberator Magazine,* or attendants on the Sunday night assemblies from Maine to California, and from Michigan to Texas, have already gained an inkling of the date's significance.

But that is not the end of the matter.

THE NEW LIBERATOR and *The League of the Liberators* have brought me into direct personal contact with many of the greatest public men in our nation. The significance of the revelations, the nature of the events lying ahead, confirmed by the trend of the times, has attracted the notice of some of our leading publicists, statesmen and industrialists. I find myself in this late summer of 1931, spending as much of my time in Washington, D. C., as at our publication offices in Manhattan. I find myself in constant consultation with a great group of advanced students of the times who see only too clearly the "gale in the wind," who know of the tremendous inroads that anti-Christ influences and factors are making upon our national life. These men are preparing to make some tangible move toward amelioration of conditions that are rapidly becoming insufferable.

This work is proceeding apace with every indication that before the new year of 1932, it will become international in scope. Already there are nearly a thousand teacher-executives or people directly or indirectly interested in spreading the Liberation Message throughout America. *The New Liberator Magazine* has better than ten thousand readers an issue, and plans are being perfected to publish it weekly.

All this work has grown with almost no missionary or promotional work on my part, mostly by word of mouth advertising on the part of those who for the first time in their lives have found, or are finding, liberation from the doubts, fears, superstitions, or inartistic misinterpretations of the old theological idea that taught men they were as the dust of the ground instead of being what Christ Himself designated them, sons of God, Christs in their own right in a sort of earthly classroom. . . .

My own part in the endeavor, however, as time goes on seems to be one of increasing practicality and the counselling of very real spiritual forces working in a practical way to bring about better relations in society. I say this without self-aggrandizement, holding no illusions about the drudgery, danger, and sacrifice entailed by the labor as it is definitely shaping for me to do in conjunction with my friends of similar enlightenment.

Those who know me intimately from daily association will attest that I have no Messianic Complex and do not for one instant assume that the salvation of the human race in these hours of its extremities, devolves upon me or any other individual. I have simply come to realize the deep personal obligation entailed by being the recipient of this material from some higher field or arena of mentality, that works such spiritual wonders when applied to the individual. I have seen far too many lives salvaged, too many souls regain their faith and confidence in a loving and constructive Deity, too many careers saved from materialistic destruction by a proper understanding of what is now "coming over" for me to doubt the inspirational character of that which I have turned over to others as fast as it has been given to me.

I know that there have incarnated in mortal bodies in this generation vast numbers of dark, satanic souls who are being literally driven down from the higher realms of light, who are massing their forces for a fresh onslaught on humankind that still has faith in, and love for, the literal Christ Jesus. *I know that there is a literal Christ Jesus who is marshalling, directing, and leading the leaders of the Forces of Light.* Stunning as the statement may sound to those hearing of this New-Day Revelation for the first time, and not aware of the great constructive agencies that are afoot, there are those among us, of great repute in this nation, men of reliability not given to hallucinations *who have confronted Him in materialized form in a manner and form not to be challenged.*

66

Looking back now over the past forty years, I can see that every bothersome circumstance in which I found myself enmeshed, every business project which I essayed and which crumbled to dust in my hands, most of the contacts I made among persons who have affected my life, have all contributed something to the equipment necessary to prosecute this greater work and carry it on to a successful fruition.

The same mentors and guides who received me that night in California are still with me, conversing with me evening on evening, although I am harkening less to the Voices now and more to *The Voice*. I find myself, without self-invitation, without any knowledge of the fact by the public, in the center and swirl of the spiritual and industrial life of the nation, counselling leaders in industry, reaching thousands of people weekly with the supernal intelligence that continues to come unerringly.

What other explanation can be put upon all this than that there is a higher world of reality, peopled by those who truly have the good of the mortal race at heart and are counselling it out of its present woes and tumults into a fairer social state "when all old things shall have passed away.". . .

AGAIN I say, it is in no spirit of bombast, or any self-elation, that I look back over the vicissitudes of the past three years and view them in the light of what I feel obligated to do with those who are about me.

For my associates have come on schedule as it was predicted and promised they would come—devout men and women—*each motivated to join in the labor by strange occurrences in their own lives, with which I had nothing to do.* Funds are accruing from equally strange quarters, from persons in many instances whom I have never met face to face. Mysteriously the mails turn up the "supply" with which to carry on and increase.

I believe the labor is The Christ's with all my heart, soul, and body, or it never could be progressing as I am witnessing it progress, day unto day and week unto week!

Humanity can only come out of its present woes and quandaries at the behest of, and by the leadership, of a great group of Christ-led men and women with a sincere love for the race in their hearts, taking orders *that are available* from higher dimensions of Time and Space, and acting upon them in concert with great influences shed upon the race by those Colossal souls who have the real destinies of the nations in charge.

It is a mighty task that we confront, but we go forward into it secured by a faith attested by the materializations of events.

III

IT WOULD not be fair to close this strange story without some sort of implication of what is coming about specifically in circumstance to augment this enlightenment in permanent form.

One week-end back in August, 1929—months before the great stock-market crash, before I had started *The New Liberator Magazine,* and while I was still answering the flood of correspondence that had accrued from publishing *"My Seven Minutes in Eternity"*—I had gone to spend Sunday with an old iron-master interested in psychical research in his home in Greenwich, Conn.

As we strolled about his estate in Sabbath twilight, he suddenly asked: "Young man, if you had a quarter-million dollars presented to you for the carrying on of your work, how would you expend it?"

His question appalled me.

I finally answered: "Frankly, I don't know. At the present time it's not clear in my mind just what the goal in this work is to be."

"But," he argued, "you seem to be getting psychical material that refers to something definite growing from your experience at some future date. I know because of what you've read me today before starting on this walk."

I said: "I have a premonition, but not of a nature to make me say definitely what I would do with a quarter-million dollars."

To be truthful, the material that was coming over to me at that time dealt with matters that I was having plenty of difficulty in accrediting myself. I was being told of a coming crash on the bourses of the world, of a period of prolonged depression that would follow—prolonged by an international group of rapacious individuals who were incarnations of dark souls in life to deliberately block and thwart the Christ and all His works in the present generation. I was being told the most intimate details of a Great Contest that was in prospect on both sides of the Veil of Life, when souls were to be divided into two great camps: Those who believed in God, and Those who did not believe in God—who would do all within their power to favor the works of the Anti-Christ the adversary.

Recorded at a time when prosperity was at its height, when our economists could not figure out the faintest chance for a depression for at least five years, I was as puzzled and skeptical about the validity of my material as anyone to whom I showed it. I was in the center of a great flood of revelation myself; I was having the final stages of my own awakening that should equip me for aiding others later with theirs, and any period of action, epitomized by a $250,000 endowment, had not yet arrived.

But I went home the next morning doing some galvanic thinking. Suppose that all I was being told *was* coming to pass!

It had been predicted in my material that within a scant two years I would be in direction of a new movement for spiritual awakening in this nation, whose adherents would run into thousands. Within three years this was to become international in scope and effect. Within five years it was to become so formidable that it would constitute one of the most effective challenges in this generation to the earth's dark atheistic forces, and eventually bringing them down to defeat.

Being as human—and I hope as balanced—as anyone reading this narrative, I was greatly perturbed. Were mischief-makers plaguing me with delusions of grandeur? Did I have a secret Messianic Complex of which I was unaware? By what miracle could I, a writer of magazine tales in a New York apartment, be raised to become a mouthpiece for a national or international "spiritual awakening" within three years?

It was all too grandiose at the time and I had to wait and see what developed. But even while pondering these predictions, I was continually getting into plights as with my iron-master friend. I was being called definitely to state my purpose and my goal. And I could not state it because it was all too vague.

I gave the matter much thought that Monday. In the evening, when the woman who worked with me transcribing the material at my dictation, came in to take down our daily instruction, I told her of my quandary.

"I am going to ask definite information of our Higher Friends," I said, "concerning where all this is bearing us and what definite goal we should keep in mind in order to talk intelligently to people like my host of yesterday."

I put my inquiry audibly, when we had prepared ourselves for writing. *Suddenly it seemed as though a magnificent vibration began to grow in that room where we sat. I felt it in my body. My companion felt it also. Someone of transcendant spirituality had come down into that apartment and was standing invisible beside us as we wrote!*

At eight o'clock in the evening we began. It was long after midnight when the transcript was ended. But before the first half-hour had passed we discerned that what was being given us was a sublime "Master Message" expounding in not-to-be-forgotten terms the scope of our brevets.

A mighty foundation was coming from this enlightenment. It was not to be as other foundations, dependant on the lengthened shadow of one man's personality or wealth to render it secure in the days that were to come. *It was to be a steady amalgamation of the Christ Forces on this planet, uniting themselves for new manifestation!*

Supplementary discourses gave me more specific details of how this foundation was to come into being, and how it would function. When I told my friends in the opening of the Assemblies for the Liberation that I had no intention of starting a new cult, I therefore knew whereof I spoke. This was to be more vital than any religious cult, bigger than any one person or set of persons. But I could not reveal it until sufficient corroborative evidence had occurred in event to make the general trend and outcome of the whole gesture creditable.

In order that those hearing of this whole experience—and its aftermath—for the first time may gain some idea of the character of the communication that has been going on for the past three years, and understand why I disclaim any charge of composition or fabrication, I print in the pages immediately following the most vital portions of the "Master Message" received that Monday evening. I have deleted those lines or expoundings that I felt were intended for me personally, that could hold no interest for general readers.

I submit this beautiful document for what it seems to be worth. Decidedly it has become a motivating factor in the establishment of the significant institution I shall speak about presently—

THE FOUNDATION MESSAGE

IV

I SAY UNTO YOU, BELOVED: Pitch your tents among the righteous; make your peace with the forsaken; raise up standards to the truth;

2.   I tell you, beloved, a Man cometh to you; He maketh a mission of life-giving in circumstance; He openeth His heart and gathereth the nations;

3.   Long have they expected Him; the prophets of old have sung of Him sweetly; He raiseth up hope in the breasts of the anointed;

4.   His mission is great among peoples of earth;

5.   He shall treat with men justly and shew them their birthright; He shall tell them the truth and it maketh them righteous.

6.   My beloved, harken to Me: *I am that Man!*

7.   I come in a chariot not drawn by beasts; I come in a radiance not seen of eye; I speak to My people and My people give heed; I speak to the nations and the nations give ear.

8.   Long have I suffered their transgressions of blindness; I suffer no more that their blindness should blind them.

9.   I speak to My people and My people know My voice; I speak to Mine anointed and Mine anointed see My face; I speak to My beloved and My beloved know My grace.

10. Harken to the promise: This is renouncement of those who do folly;

11. Even as of old I said *Peace* when there was no peace, *Joy* when there was no joy, *Love* where love prevailed not, so cometh One who sayeth to you now: *The mountains are opened, the truth gusheth forth! hear ye My servants for verily they manifest! they say to you Peace!*

12. Bind up your wounds, ye nations! treat with the circumspect in your thoughts and your actions! give heed to him who suffereth, give joy to him who thirsteth!

13. Peace and contentment are the allotments of eternity; enjoyment of earth is the heritage of species.

14. Ether hath made Matter cycle raised on cycle; peoples have risen and peoples have fallen; peoples have been given high accretions of knowledge;

15. Lo, they have not benefited; each time have they misused that which hath been given them.

16. Mankind hath demanded a higher resting-place in knowledge; each time, My beloved, his malfeasance hath destroyed him.

17. Cosmic principles have come to him times beyond counting; each time he hath spurned them or used them wrongly in his thinking.

18. *Now cometh the closing of a cycle to earth!*

II

HARKEN TO MY VOICE: I come bringing water, I come bearing food.

2.   Take these for your principles:

3.   *We seek to serve humankind in ways that suffice it in pleasurable enjoyment of fiats eternal.*

4.   *We do errands of mercy to mankind the sufferer.*

5.   *We open doors of understanding to those who know not God.*

6.   *We open doors of peace to those who know not Christ.*

7.   Further we do not; this is our mission, our joy, and our reward.

III

MY BELOVED, HEAR MY VOICE: Go ye forth into the market-places and say: "The Lord hath need of substance!"

2.   Thus do ye say it:

3.   We build a firmer temple of truth than man hath known to date;

4.   We make no mock of principles celestial;

5.   We enjoin the times with deeds of mercy;

6. We open the storehouses of men's characters and find hidden therein the measures of truth;

7. We go from land to land seeking out those with the sign on their foreheads, saying unto them: "Lo, ye are wise! make known, we beseech you, that which ye know without fear or fawning, testing your principles on the rock of great utterance, standing on that rock and speaking your knowledge; stand forth and speak it; give utterance to it mightily; come forth with truth, let the nations behold it!"

8. I say to you, beloved, the nations shall behold it.

IV

HEAR YE MY MESSAGE: Give heed to the voice of Him who exalteth: "I have found the Light!"

2. Is he not of the Host that hath come into flesh?

3. Ask of the nations: "Where are your ennobled ones? open their mouths and give their speech utterance; plant firmly on the highlands the banners of your merit; concern yourselves with treasure that no man overturneth!"

4. Go forth among the nations, preach to them of hope, of brotherly concernment.

5. *Join ye the nations in a thrall of understanding.*

6. Take note of their leaders who stand on the heights that they be the anointed who minister with service.

7. Hear ye My message: Rigor is needed to make speech to the dark ones; force is required to coop their iniquities.

8. *They shall be curbed from making more mischiefs!*

9. Rigorous indeed be thy thoughts toward the debased; lift them up bodily; seize them with hands and make them surefooted, even in the light that scorcheth as it blindeth;

10. *But transmit no chord, however worthy, that containeth not the beauty of the sanctity of love!*

11. Sing no anthem, My beloved, that hath not in its music the delight of the anointed.

12. Say this unto men: "Lo, the times have come on you when man shall know that he standeth or falleth by his own intestines strengthened with mercy!"

13. He goeth forth to battle; perceiveth he that he warreth against his own species?

14. *Make him to see it!*

15. Say unto him: "Keep a great peace, live a great joy, do a great deed!"

16. The times have arrived for man to know ennoblement; they are ripe with understanding; harken not to the sluggard who faileth to hear the voice from the dawn that hovereth on the hilltop.

17. Say this unto man: "All over the earth are scattered a host that maketh rejoicings that the goodly times be imminent";

18. Know ye these persons: bring them together.

19. Perceive ye not that a great mission hath been instituted among men in this generation?

20. *Organize ye the spirits of God, not in worldly form as armies led by earthly chieftains, but rather as a kingly host, each chamberlain having within himself a vassal.*

21. Give heed to those who cry: "Behold that we perish in that light cometh not!"

22. Lo, perish they not; do we save them with much radiance.

23. Give heed to those who cry: "Sustenance we demand, for our worldly souls are famished on the husks of benevolent instructions having in them no wisdom!"

24. Open your arms to those who come saying: "Use us for the truth's sake!"

25. Give ear to those who say: "We would serve our Lord gladly if we but knew our ministration!"

26. Give thought to those who exalt: "Let us sing a goodly anthem, for we have had revealed to us the nature of the kingly ones who do come to minister unto us!"

V

THESE THINGS I TELL YOU, MY BELOVED: Go ye forth into the world and say: "The Lord hath set ministers in each land and clime; He seeketh their ennoblement to raise them; let their missions know fulfillment without hindrance from trying circumstance!"

2.   Go ye forth to the nations and say: "Give us of your best ones, O ye lands, that they gather in a body and rebuke the unanointed!"

3.   Gather to yourselves your helpers;

4.   Strike out boldly;

5.   *Plow your furrow!*

6.   These are the matters awaiting your hands.

7.   God hath a goodly mission for the pure in heart; they do stand upon street-corners now and implore the passing throngs; presently they shall stand upon battlements and hurl down the legions that do march against pure doctrine.

8.   Presently come to you chamberlains of finance bearing goodly gifts; thus treat ye with them:

9.   "We gather for a purpose, gentlemen of affluence, under the banner of One who hath sent forth His fiat: *All is of instruction!*

10.   "We come seeking earthly ways and means of making the ignorant see the banners of truth approaching and know of their significance;

11. "We study ways and means of righteous dealings with the nations, not being as students at petty parables and charms, but as strong men looking on life as a problem to be solved in equity, each man to his neighbor;

12. "We seek a conclave of mighty souls who preach of truth to the nations of men, each one from his mountain height, and rally the hosts of His earthly ministers into concrete activity that is accredited of men;

13. "We seek no humble lot for these are great professions;

14. "We say unto men: The times are on us when the goodly souls of every land must share their heritage in common;

15. "We come bearing gifts among the races, bespeaking the loud word *Peace!* that the warlike meet their Conqueror, that all who suffer may know release;

16. "This is our mission, gentlemen of affluence!"

VI

SPEAK YE FURTHER TO THE CHAMBERLAINS: "We go into every land and clime and behold the needs of the world's forgotten;

2. "We publish them abroad among the righteous and offer them love in place of tumults;

3. *"We send them ships of supply instead of armaments; we send them vessels loaded with mercy instead of guns to level their homesteads!*

4.   "We stand forth boldly, saying: The times have come for rigorous education of the multitude, not in concepts or precepts, but in mighty visions of eternal truths manifesting in all men's hearts.

5. "The nations, we say, have a gift in common: Peace and Understanding of Why Life Should Be So;

6.   "We treat with them, gentlemen, finding in each nation the learned ones, the young men, to whom is given the knowledge of the Life That Is To Be when warfare shall have ceased and men have known their heritage.

7. "This is our mission: *Peace! Mercy! Knowledge!* the tenets of understanding, the planks in the eternal platform of love!"

8.   Say this mightily to the nations in every land and clime: we seek the enlightened; we say to them:

9. *"How best can ye serve those who are about you, taking no thought for yourselves, manifesting no hope that is not of knowledge of the truth within yourselves, leading each man to the fountain-head of knowledge as it pleaseth him?"*

10.   We make a world shibboleth of this, our program: Peace!— Mercy!—Knowledge!—all given us for *giving!*

VII

MY BELOVED, I CHARGE YE WITH A CHARGE: Out of the mouths of those who suffer cometh a cry to the halls of affluence.

2. Do ye readjust the balance!

3. Give unto him that rejoiceth with you, that he may rejoice the more in thanksgiving that ye are in your flesh, in My name ministering.

4. Take this with you to your conclaves, wheresoever they may be.

5. The Lord hath called every man in his own right, even as ye have been called, My beloved; him will ye know by the sign on his forehead;

6. Use him as it pleaseth you; turn ye his hands to the handles of the plow;

7. Give him of your wisdom;

8. *Rebuke him not for error but praise him for the depths of beauty found within his soul!*

9. Use him, I say unto you, knowing that it will be well with you in your wisdom *how* to use him.

10. Ye are called to do a goodly work in this, My vineyard; the laborers await, each one for his hire, being eager to labor, each one at his price.

11. That price is knowledge.

12. Pay it to him richly, pressed down and overflowing; treat with him according to his talents and let him be known as an employee of the Host.

13. For verily that he is, till the goodly days are ended.

14. I speak as one, beloved, who hath an understanding.

15. Hosts of men come to you and ask of you assistance; treat with them mightily; thus make speech to them:

16. "What canst thou do in the land wherein thou dwellest, to raise that land to a knowledge of the Godhead in peace, supply, and wisdom?"

17. Treat not with him that sayeth: "I am of the Host already, for do I not pray daily for deliverance from mine error?"

18. Say unto him: "And what doest thou whilst thou prayest, or afterward?"

19. Consider the ways of those who till the soil even of humanity; what seed sow they? have they knowledge of cosmic truth? have they knowledge of eternal principles? have they knowledge of ether and its manifestations? or sow they seeds of bitterness, of strife, of petty malfeasance and injurious attraction, one nation toward the other?

20. Question those who come to you; ask of them their wisdom; ask of them their vision; translate to them the knowledge which ye have and observe their bickerings when ye have expressed yourselves.

21. Is it not true that they will say unto you: "These are your concepts; lo, we have others equally as great!"

22. Know, My beloved, that they are workers of confusions; they have not the wisdom;

23. The wisdom sayeth: All men are brethren;

24. *Only one truth is permitted to men: that they shall love, and love, and love again.*

25. Tell ye them this and observe their concernments.

26. If sobeit they say unto you: "These things we know and rejoice at!" take them into your arms and your bosoms; make them of merit in your company, manifesting to them all the sweet joys of fellowship, treating not with them as slaves but as brethren, opening your coffers and giving them supply.

27. Tedious, tedious, are the wanderings of the souls that seek for wisdom; tedious, tedious, are the wonderings of the souls that seek for leaders.

28. Say not unto them: "Behold us, your leaders!" say unto them rather: "Ye are leaders in your own rights where it be that ye may travel."

29. Say unto each man: "Lead thou in thy chosen circle and in thy leadership be great."

30. For leadership hath a quality that sayeth: "Go ye and manifest; I do follow to protect you."

31. Seek not him who sayeth: "I am leader of the present," but seek him who sayeth to you rather: "I am searcher after knowledge."

32. Tell him that searching marketh him for leadership under the Captain whose banner is service.

33. The Captain awaiteth without, seeking His followers not in halls of revelation so much as in the byways of silent hunting after treasure.

34. Tell him who asketh of you for leadership: "Thou art leader in thine own right, arise and execute the commission given thee; for who hath better right to lead than he who sayeth: "Master, I follow and take others with me!"

35. *I bid you take My company and lead it to a high, high place where all nations see your benevolence marking you out as captains of service, verily, verily, till your earthly days be ended.*

36. Catch ye the vision? act ye upon it!

37. See ye the tapestry resplendent with colors? make it a carpet for your goings, that your feet may tread joyously and the end be fulfillment.

38. When the goodly days shall come, then shall men rally around those who have taught them to pray: Our Father, who art in heaven, give us of Thy wisdom;

39. Give us this day our daily illumination to light the way of feet that do falter;

40. Give us this day not our daily bread but bread for those who hunger more than we do;

41. Lead us not back into quagmires of ignorance for such is not Thy nature, but send us ennoblement that we may manifest our dignity, our wisdom, and our vision, to unborn generations;

42. Peace and a goodly heritage be upon the nations; this our prayer we pray in tranquility that those who say it after us may live it in their intercourse!

VIII

I BID YOU RISE UP AND KNOW THAT I ADDRESS YOU: It behooveth you to know that a goodly company awaiteth its captains, awaiting them long in the byways of service.

2. Peace! I say unto you; a goodly prospect awaiteth your vision.

3. Abide ye in the faith that maketh the race a race to be run for the sake of the running, not for awards bestowed at the goal.

4. What need have ye of more than this, beloved?

5. Peace be unto you and the little band awaiting you, making you to shine as meteors when the skies are full of darkness.

6. Presently I go to the Father who sayeth: "What of the earth and the peoples thereon?"

7. Then make I reply: "The times and the seasons are ripe for achievement: the goal is in sight and the running Ennoblement."

8. Rejoice and be exceeding glad, ye who run with Me; for we have made promises each to the other, that maketh that ennoblement a prospect in reality.

9. Choose ye whom ye will serve, ye peoples, God or Mammon! lo your service marketh you forever.

10. So let it be till the evil days are ended.

11. Come I to all of you in due cycle of event; not in spirit but literally;

12. For My spirit ye have always!

13. I pronounce on you My Peace! . .

V

SUCH WAS the sublime document—or what I choose to hold as a sublime document—that first crystallized my thinking into making a definite gesture toward the amalgamation of a Great Christ Force, international in scope, that should throw the gauntlet to the satanic influences now seeking the perversion of our current civilization.

As I have previously written, I have neither the time nor the space to rehearse here the auxiliary and supplementary discourses recorded over thirty months that have clarified the instruments and agencies, the means and the methods, by which this International Christ Force could make itself a juggernaut in the present generation.

In my secular pursuits and investigations I have come to the conclusion that *the Christ people of Christendom do not know their own strength!* If they knew their own power to act in concert for true righteousness, their sufferings would be ended.

They are lost in a maze of erroneous teachings, hoodwinked by false leaders who deceive or default on them when those leaders stand to gain in personal profit, unable to obtain the pure instruction—even from secular sources—necessary to free them from their fears and doubtings.

Evil men, using instruments and agencies that no Christ Person can employ, conspire to hold them in an economic bondage, debauching intellect and the public press into accepting that such economic bondage is beyond all the factors in human control. The truth of the stupendous beauties Behind Life in Mortality is besmeared and befouled by heathenish doctrine that it savors of diabolism to probe for reality or learn of existence in its postmortem aspects.

These things I have realized, not only from my own transcendant "studies" but from people sent to me on schedule, exactly as it was predicted to me psychically that they would come, who had wide worldly knowledge of what was transpiring beneath mundane affairs.

At the same time I have come to realize that the moment I became in any wise a power that challenged the capacity of the Beast in these earthly agencies, *no amount of effort, money, or social pressure would be spared to discredit and besmirch me, to suppress or silence me!*

In this day of great publicity agencies controlled or intimidated by utterless selfish forces, it is only necessary to criminally libel and besmut one who suddenly rears above the heads of the crowd with a new message of liberation, to deal him a death-blow and render him impotent. There is rarely any redress from such agencies of publicity. Once you seriously threaten the domination of these dark, selfish, atheistic forces, you are marked for swift elimination.

I know of one outstanding case, fully documented, of a brave, beautiful, and patriotic woman who nearly succeeded in building a national organization to combat these atheistic forces in the political and industrial life of our nation. She was gaining to a power that threatened the complete exposure and destruction of the diabolical "boring from within" influences seeking at this very moment to undermine the foundations of our government.

What happened?

Backed by millions of money, these satanic interests succeeded in having a false photograph of her distributed throughout the news pages of the nation, with a *wholly fabricated* account of her alleged indiscretions, making her out a dangerous adventuress subtly in the employ of the various agencies she was successfully combating. She brought criminal libel suit against the newspapers that had so besmirched her. But that suit was mischievously dragged along *for four years,* exhausting her finances and breaking her health. Finally her following, unable to hear her side of the story or accredit the diablerie arranged against her, accepted the accusations made in the press. She was forthwith discredited. Her power disintegrated. At the end of the four years she won her suit for vindication, *the jury giving her a verdict of one cent and the papers that had lent themselves to her destruction printing six-line retractions on their inside pages among their advertisements!*

And it broke her heart and killed her.

I have learned, not from psychical sources so much as secular contacts among the forces making for law and order in the nation, that the very size and might of these dark forces renders them chimerical to the average person. And thus the campaign of intimidation goes on. Those who cannot be used unwittingly as a "front" for their operations, are debauched financially, criminally blackmailed, or in the last analysis mysteriously destroyed.

Many have commented upon the fact that there has been little or no publicity in the nation's press concerning this inception of the League for Liberation. I have purposely avoided and discouraged all such till I got my plans completed—or advanced to a point—*where the work could pyramid and grow into an unstoppable juggernaut irrespective of the attacks that might be launched at me personally.*

I do not expect wholly to escape them. I have been told psychically that they would come, and something of their nature. I should not be surprised to see a campaign of intimidation against my associates in the field mysteriously begin—religious interests being used as the blind tool of these satanic forces to embarrass these associates. Attacks against my personal character and sanity will probably come. It is psychically predicted, not alone by my own mentors but through other sensitives, that three attempts will be made on my life.

I can look at the whole campaign of vileness and vituperation with equanimity, however. *I know the year that I am going back onto the Other Side to remain for good with the work completed, and how I am to go!* The old saying, "A man destined to die of the cholera cannot be hanged as a horse thief," has a cryptic application to my own life.

Nevertheless, having taken this mission very seriously now because of the proofs in circumstances that have come again and again on schedule, I have a certain respect for the grimness of the contest to be waged. And to make the distress as small as possible, I have tried to minimize my own importance insofar as I could in the work's initial stages.

There are now thousands of people who have been faithfully attending Liberator Assemblies week after week, reading *The New Liberator magazine* month after month, who have accepted that I have merely been completing this chain of assemblies as I edited my magazine.

Many others who are affluent have sincerely desired to donate large sums of money for the growth of this movement but who have been hesitant, or kept silent, knowing that injury to me, or my elimination, might mean the loss of all that they presented.

But throughout the past year—I am completing this re-write of *The Aftermath to Seven Minutes in Eternity* in early September, 1931—I have been assiduously working not to found a new religious cult, or another sectarian denomination, but to project this new doctrine on an educational and academic basis!

It is time to make the nation-wide announcement that there has come into potential existence what amounts to A GREAT CHRISTIAN UNIVERSITY—THE COLLEGE OF CHRISTIAN ECONOMY AND SCHOOL OF COMPARATIVE RELIGIONS!

WE HAVE had Domestic Economy, we have had Political Economy.

Why have we never had Christian Economy or the Science of Applying the Principles and Precepts of the Christ to the Mundane Circumstance?

During this summer of 1931 a benefactress in Manhattan has made a tender of 100 acres of mountain land in one of our Atlantic States. On this property—if the Plan is not changed by Higher Agencies—despite the Depression that is now upon the nation, in the teeth of all opposition and obstruction because I believe the work is being motivated by agencies above human influence, those who have caught the vision from the private documents and discourses I have shown them, will go forward with the construction of buildings of beauty, *wherein shall be taught all those courses of enlightenment now rigorously opposed or suppressed by those worldly systems that stand to lose caste by Real Truth becoming known!*

A great instructional body, a great publishing plant, a great gathering-place for the finest Christian minds of the earth, will be brought into existence and function in times sadly in want of what they have to give in the spirit of Christ-Service.

It is necessary to have a safe and permanent repository for the original versions of such manuscripts as offered in this monograph several pages back.

It is necessary to have a postgraduate course where those who wish to prepare themselves for making this teaching their lifework may gather together under competent instructors and be privately taught what cannot be revealed to the crowd as a mass.

There is a necessity for a great investigational body that shall truthfully and sincerely delve into the religious records of the past and bring to light without fear or favor the error in the doctrines that have plunged humanity into this cruel hiatus of Christian belief.

There is a necessity for a university body that shall forthwith investigate psychical phenomena as it deserves to be investigated—in constructive psychology—exploring behind life on a basis of belief in survival instead of disbelief and seeking to demonstrate that all "sensitives" are charlatans.

There is a necessity for a great quasi-medical fraternity that shall study and explore the phenomena of subjective insanity, equipping and qualifying physicians and psychiatrists, and the heads of institutions dealing with lunacy in all its forms, to treat with obsessions and possessions by accrediting the existence of malign discarnate forces.

There is a necessity for a great educational institution that shall preach, not a Christ dead by crucifixion, *but a Christ Alive and Dominant in the economic and industrial affairs of men,* thwarting the dark, destructive, atheistic forces of this nation and all nations in their anti-Christ activities.

There is a necessity for an institution promulgating these enlightenments, that cannot be debauched or controlled by secular worldly interests, with a charter so drawn that no persons can gain to power within its directorate who are not American citizens by birth, of proven Christian faith, incapable of being intimidated, with militant ideals of sobriety and integrity working to make personal honesty and circumspect conduct popular again in the Body Politic!

There are millions of Christian people in this country of every creed who are tired of the false, the base, the untrue. They hunger for a return to the high ideals, the clean behaviorism, the personal reliability of their fathers who made this nation great. They do not want any return to an intolerant Puritanism or sanctimonious theology. They want a standard of living raised before them that shall overwhelm and drive to cover all those disintegrating influences in our national life that are cheapening their culture and debauching their offspring.

The psychological time has arrived for a reflex swing of the pendulum of society into constructive, ennobling channels, that the honest man may know his antagonist, that the honest religionist may distinguish his God. A chaotic but titanic mass of Christian Americans is ready to answer to a battle cry that means the end of gunplay in our streets, spoliation of our daughters, the defilement of our homes, the undermining of our government—all by the instrumentalities and financings of forces avowedly atheistic, haters of the Christ and all His works, who declare that they will have Christian humanity groveling on its knees within this generation.

Praise God there are those whose eyes are being opened.

They know the challenge of The Beast.

That challenge they accept!

ONLY a dominant Christian institution that stands four-square behind the Man of Galilee, that presents a rallying point for those vast constructive forces, that epitomizes an oscillation back to decency and honor without sanctimony or loss of that sense of humor that is always the lubricant of the spirit of love, can deal effectively with these problems of our times.

Humbly and contritely, as God gives me strength and acumen, as I hear The Voice in silence, *I propose to found such an institution within the coming autumn!*

I propose to make every Liberator Assembly in every city and town throughout this nation a weekly Extension Course for those who cannot attend such a school in person.

Every Liberator Assembly in America, no matter how large, no matter how small, I propose to make a living, breathing, dynamic force for constructive Christian Idealism in its community, throwing behind each one all the enlightenment, all the erudition, all the gleanings from deep research and investigatory work that such a university can command and direct, offering the humblest Christian seeker in the smallest hamlet that wealth of unbiased, uncolored learning for which his soul is famished.

I hope it is no delusion of grandeur of which I am guilty in suddenly realizing that my psychical material has proven its validity in secular event, and that this is the lifework to which I am called—the vague, intangible, but irrepressible brevet to which I felt myself headed when I registered with my editorial friends years ago that tapping out fiction stories on a typewriter was not the job I had entered life to do. It was just under the threshold of consciousness then, tormenting me. Now it has all come clear.

I know this project is to become a reality because I am already in touch with the men and women who will make it a reality. They have not only assured me of their loyalty and support, but in many cases persons of great erudition and importance politically, industrially, religiously and socially, have already foregone attractive worldly offers to consecrate the remainder of their lives to this ideal. My plans have come to that stage of fruition where—even were I discredited or eliminated tomorrow—the founding of this institution would go onward to actuality.

And no power on earth or from hell can stop or alter that which is thus decreed by these Higher Forces, gathering this clan to perform this worthy office.

It is not a church that I seek to found, but a *University of the Future,* a university whose students shall go out over all the earth and "organize the Spirits of God, not in worldly form as armies led by earthly chieftains, but rather as a kingly host, each chamberlain having within himself a vassal!" . . .

I am taking my commission seriously in this: that an organization can be perfected so self-supporting that it solicits no funds from the coffers of Mammon, so inspired by direct contact with those above the earthly predicament that its ministrations shall be felt to the ends of the earth.

I say I have tenders of service from men and women of erudition, adepts each one in his or her line, to staff such a college: Christian people of unquestioned loyalty to the American Ideal without fanaticism, without race prejudices, without obligations that make them vulnerable to intimidating influences. I know that Great Forces *that have proven themselves in my own affairs* are operating behind the lives of these men and women to turn their talents to this labor and make its Extension possible with millions of money. And those same Forces are awakening the possessors of that money, making them realize that their wealth has never been their own but was put in their hands in trust for this spiritual enhancement of the peoples of our times.

It is no smug academic institution that I would found. I would start no school that hides itself and its students away from the world to advance the tenets of some freakish doctrine. *I would project a living, forceful, dynamic organization of Christ-Workers in a new social order, that will make each of the present Liberator Assemblies or Study Classes a contact point for its work among the masses.*

It will train men and women in all those studies and sciences now considered forbidden in orthodox institutions seeking to uphold an archaic social fabric.

And most of the instruction promulgated thus, would continue to come from the sources from which has come the instruction to the assemblies up to the present. . . .

VI

AND THIS is the undeleted story, and the real significance of the episode that has been publicized throughout the globe as *"My Seven Minutes in Eternity."*

My dear friend Will Levington Comfort, the novelist, has been generous enough to acclaim the whole experience as "the story of the Age." Perhaps! I do not know. I am still too close to it—there is still too much work to be done.

Insofar as the discarnate part of the experience was concerned, let no one draw the conclusion that contact with these higher forces is impossible unless one is chosen to write a book, publish a magazine or found a college. I know too many hundreds of people, in all walks of life, who have had the same colossal adventure—who have established the same communication—and who have no call to do more than apply the profits resulting to their individual lives and experiences.

But in my own case, step by step, denouement by denouement, this work has grown. And now I am coming to see that every experience which I underwent in life prior to that night in California, every business venture that seemed to turn out abortive, every personal contact I made with persons of every type of mentality, *all happened specifically to give me an additional bit of equipment for that labor which now looms.*

I recall that at one time I was especially disgruntled that I had been drawn into the ownership and management of a chain of restaurants in Southern California. Why on earth, I wondered, should I have become embroiled in a restaurant proposition—which diverted my attention from more important activities and cost me no small amount of money. One night in my communicating, I asked. The answer came back: "To give you an education in feeding people in large numbers in situations that are yet in the future!" And so it has gone. . . .

Money, talent, and property, is now coming in from all quarters of the country, to make this epochal enterprise an overwhelming success. The weird phase of these gifts in many instances is *that many of the donors are "sensitives" themselves who declare they have been acquainted with this work, and the validity of the agencies behind it in other dimensions of Matter, by voices that have spoken directly to them, advising them to become connected with it, with least possible delay.*

Those who accuse me of commercializing my awakened senses in the aftermath of the experience, are speaking from a lack of knowledge of me or the facts. When I lay down to sleep that night in California three years ago, I had a comfortable little estate that figured up in the neighborhood of $100,000—property, securities, business interests and cash. I had a writing vocation that paid me something like $25,000 a year. The losses I have since taken, directly traceable to the disruption of pulling up stakes in California and coming East to devote my life to this enterprise, have consumed every dollar of my estate — even plunged me in debt. My earning power as a writer has totally vanished, due to the fact that most popular publishers are fearful of stirring up the mare's nest of interest which *The American Magazine* stirred up by printing literary material over my name. If it is not material similar to *"My Seven Minutes in Eternity"* their readers are disappointed and disgruntled. If it is similar, they are in for a deluge that they would not invite.

There is not the slightest self-pity or regret in the statement that from an earning capacity of $25,000 a year, I have dropped to a revenue of about $35 a week, taken out of the receipts from the work for my personal living expenses.

That much for "commercializing" my abnormal "talents."

I am giving my life now to another type of work entirely. And I am radiantly happy in so doing. I have found the thing that lay just under the threshold of my consciousness for so many years and caused me so many midnights of heartburn.

Perhaps after another three years has passed, I shall re-write *The Aftermath to Seven Minutes in Eternity* again. In another three years I may have personal experiences and developments to add which make this foregoing account puerile and inane.

I know that what I am doing now constitutes a glorious adventure that can only be a constructive gesture in our advancing civilization.

Certainly no university of this age, or any other age, has attempted to carry subdivisions of itself into the cities, towns, and hamlets of the country in which it exists, calling people of limited means together in great masses to hear the latest reports of its findings and instruct them in the latest developments of scientific Christian truth.

No great university of this age, or any other age, has opened its doors to those who simply want instruction in the Great Facts Behind Life, irrespective of their years or previous academic schooling.

It is a University of the New Order that my associates would aid me in projecting, welding into a sensible reality all those constructive agencies in society that make for a higher Christian Idealism, devoid of theological limitations, looking at life as a problem to be solved in equity, each man to his neighbor.

We shall try to bring to humankind *the Christ-Force in action,* going out into the highways and byways among all nations, "seeking the Enlightened ones, the young men, to whom is given a knowledge of the Life That Is to Be when warfare shall have ceased and men have known their heritage."

But it is not another pacifist society—that would usher in peace by serving banquets—that is now in process of erection. No participation is asked in councils of nations while those councils are in any way dominated or intimidated by the dark souls ensconced in mortal flesh.

We come in clean, frank patriotism—in selfless devotion to the One Who Knew Gethsemane—in high, fine confidence in a God who knows and rules the nations—and without fanaticism, in sober sense and logic, offer our lives to a Monument of Intellect erected to world fellowship purged of the adversary.

And we overlook not, nor maximize, the final lines of the Master Message that first sent this gesture into crystallized form—

"So be it till the evil days are ended. Come I to all of you in due cycle of event, not in spirit but literally, *for My spirit ye have always!*"

I aver that I know it.

I have lived, as I am living now, for a time in eternity!

(Excerpts and photographs from Pelley's autobiography, The Door to Revelation, published in 1939)

THE EARLY YEARS

This is the story of a man who spent the first thirty-eight years of his life groping for something higher and more satisfying than the normal rewards from strictly worldly living. Then in the thirty-ninth year of his age, in a single night, without the slightest suggestion of a warning, something happened as he lay asleep that altered his career, his philosophy, his destiny. It is also the story of a man who sought to share what came from that experience with millions of his fellow mortals stumbling in bogs of spiritual perplexity, academic fallacy, political subversion and economic bedlam..... and how they received it, and what later grew out of it.

I once knew a woman who owned a puppy. She lived in a house in torrid New York. She became so solicitous of her pet that one summer she sought a place in the country where her poodle could romp to its small heart's content. After going to the trouble of making the journey, she set the dog down on a five-acre lawn. With a pat and a push, she stood up to watch it gambol. But did that pooch gambol? Indeed, it did not. It took one look at those awful open spaces and streaked for a hole beneath the nearby veranda. And it stayed in that hole, I might say, doggedly. No amount of coaxing throughout the remainder of that visit could persuade it to come forth. That dog was born in confinement and would not be satisfied with anything but confinement. It did not really want light and freedom. When freedom was offered, it scurried for confinement in nice cozy darkness.

There are humans like that, alas millions of humans. They yelp and howl behind the window panes of life, indicating that the crux of mortal bliss is escaping social dictates, or the vigilance of tutors who truly are but parrots for what wiser men have taught them. Offer them true spiritual freedom, or the chance to gambol in wholly new arenas of thought and labor, and they snap at the hand of him who would release them, or consider as menaces those who invite them to know Life as something other than darkened holes beneath structures of orthodoxy.

Going back to the start of things, where all good stories should begin, I first realized that I was again on earth, with a new body for me to occupy and a fresh life-span ahead for me to live, in a little white-box parsonage on a country road in North Prescott, Massachusetts. I do not mean that I was born there. It was nearly two years after my birth at 32 Goodrich Street, in the city of Lynn, Massachusetts, that I suddenly realized that I was human and alive. My first observations of life that impressed themselves upon my mind and caused me to marvel at the mortal status in which I now found myself, began in that parsonage beside a country church. My father was pastor in that church. I was his only son—between two and three years old.

He was a very young and earnest pastor, my father, in the Methodist denomination. He was very pink in his aquiline face, as I remember him first in those far-off years, very slim in his build, and took a vast amount of pride in the assumption that the Tribe of Pelley could trace its genealogy back in an unbroken line to one Sir John Pelley, knighted and sponsored by Good Queen Elizabeth which attested, of course, that the Pelleys were English.

For reasons that seemed sufficient to the sovereign and my forebear, he towered high enough above the rabble to be requested to kneel down. Whereupon it is logical that Queen Bess borrowed a handy cutlass from some sneering cavalier and did for the first time—of record—what many excellent women have been doing ever since: namely, took a couple of good clouts at a Pelley while she had one down. Whether Sir John had the urge to clout her back is something that is nowhere made clear in the text. I assert that he could not have been a real Pelley, however, if he had not felt it. We may let the matter pass....

So here was I, in the third year of my age, toddling on small, unsteady legs around the sun-baked foundations of a little New England church. I came into consciousness of myself that first drowsy summer, picking up bits of red and blue glass from about those foundations, as lawless youths from former years had done damage to the stained-glass windows. In the year 1892 a boggle-eyed boy on legs somewhat bowed hunted bits of colored glass about the masonry of his father's country church, or slipped the rope with which he was tied to a front-yard pear tree down about his ankles and ran away down the road to a neighbor's.... where he was served with cookies and questions, and later marched home to bed and a spanking.

It was a very lonely spot, the location of that dusty wayside church. On the eastern side of the parsonage stretched a graveyard. There was no other house in sight.... About that graveyard I thought a lot about. It was a very pleasant place in which to play, among those mossy headstones, finding berries in the brambles along its hoary fences. But when on week-day afternoons I saw the buggies of farmer folk draw up around the church, or when the weather beaten sheds in the rear had been filled with stamping horses, and after strange services for the midweek our neighbors brought out a long, black, cloth-covered box from the church's sacrosanct interior, toted it slowly up the road, and bore it in among the senile headstones, I knew a Nameless Horror.

What was contained in those heavy narrow boxes that made our parishioners act so stricken and constrained? Why were they always that dull unglistening black? I appealed to my mother. She always said, "Hush!" and cast a glance at father...

Two or three years later, down in the village of East Templeton, an older girl named Carrie "passed over" suddenly. I had played with this Carrie. We had squatted under the same huge umbrella when a summer shower caught us off in a pasture. I recalled that intimacy as her funeral cortege wound slowly up the hill before the house, with fourteen whiffletrees creaking musically and steel tires striking small rocks in the sand. A matronly neighbor, delegated to keep me at home while my parents held the services, told me that Carrie was in the long black box that I could see through the glass of the carriage at the front.

What had happened to Carrie? I had known of her brief illness and vaguely understood it. But what did they mean by "dead" and how could she move in that mystical black box? I watched the procession move up out of sight. Carrie was gone ....and yet I cannot say truthfully that I did not know what was passing before me. Searching my memory honestly as I write these lines, it seems that in those far-off years I was quite as old a person as I feel myself to be at present. There were two souls of me inside.... that was how it was! One knew all things. The other asked questions.

I cannot recall that I felt any sorrow at Carrie's mystical passing. I missed her as a playmate, but deep within my heart I understood that it had to be, that the world into which I had come was scheduled that way, that down some distant year—a millennium then in eternity—I too would be ridden up a country hill in a somber vehicle with plate glass sides, lying unfeeling and motionless within. But I knew too that when that time came, movement would mean nothing. The real I would be.... away!

At the gigantic age of three, however, I was merely an ancient entity being ridden about the New England hills by two serious young adults, visiting strange families in bucolic sanctimony, exploring strange pantries, and being offered strange cookie jars. As we drove home late each night, I looked up at high stars drowsily. I heard the tugs slapping measuredly against shafts of the buggy, the creaking of the whiffletree, the clicking of tires in the sand, or the soft warm rumble of the planking as we crossed some country bridge.

At the end of those two years father received a "call" to a larger parish in East Templeton—still in Massachusetts. The town was bigger, the church was bigger, so too was the parsonage. This last was a gaunt, two-story house set behind lugubrious pines that moaned softly when the wind swished through them on rainy autumn nights. You know how pine trees might be—great Norway pines—standing before a parsonage in a bleak New England village…

They spoke strangely to me, those pine trees, on a hundred restless twilights, just before oil lamps were lit. They were striving to tell me something that vaguely reminded me of…. Carrie!

A more wholesome man than my father never lived He was clean in his thinking, he was clean in his living. He had his peculiarities, indeed who has not? He aroused my ire on a hundred times when I had become a normal young American going about life's business on my

108

own. But neither blood taint nor soul taint did he ever bequeath me. For that I can overlook our lesser dissensions.

The Pelleys had been clean living, deeply religious people ever since the first Pelley set foot on Newfoundland. Mayhap that North Atlantic storm took all of the worldliness out of the runaway Pelley and set him on land aptly frightened at God.

In her religious scruples and conscientious living, mother equaled father. If either of them erred in my early upbringing, it was by giving me an overdose of personal and domestic sanctimony, painful but guileless. Still, people took their religion seriously up in New England fifty years ago. And besides, my father was a minister. I, his son, had to measure to my role.

At just what life period father "got religion" I have never been advised. I believe his age was fourteen years when his parents brought him down here to "the States" and he started to work in the shoe shops of Lynn. He was foreman of the Valpey & Anthony stitching room when he met and married mother. They set up a modest home on Henry Avenue, in Lynn, moving later into Goodrich Street, where I was inducted into a new mortal coil at seven minutes to one o'clock on the morning of March 12, 1890. Let astrologers do with that date what they will...

Looking back now on those years, I recall that my attitude and angle on this new life in which I found myself, comprised many items that were never quite accounted for in my father's fundamentalism. In the first place, according to modern psychologists, no infant is supposed to think or remember until it has acquired a language to think or remember in. This is not true. Without meaning to publicize myself as unduly precocious, time and again after reaching maturity I recounted to mother the exact geography of the Goodrich Street rooms from which she and father moved before I was aged six months. I have told her of the steepness of the stair-flight down from upper bedrooms, the patterns of the carpets on the floors, of the short narrow hallway opening to the parlor, of the great easel with its painting of dogwood blossoms in a frame of orange plush that stood in a corner. I recalled to her the twin vases of glutinous whiteness that stood near either end of the parlor mantel holding the tail feathers from some long-denuded peacock. I remember as well the "air castle" made from bristles tied with pink yarn that hung from the ceiling and was supposed to be something very swank in the furnishing of parlors before the opening of this century.

I have a distinct recollection, too, of journeying on my back in the depths of my carriage, feeling very hot, stuffy and annoyed at my helpless inconvenience as I gazed up at the grey silk lining of the vehicle's parasol suspended above me on nickel-plated arm. I recall a day in a high wind when my carriage blew from mother's grasp, bringing it up against a fence and spilling me out . . . with no worse effects than bloodying my nose.

The strange part of those memories has been that I seemed to know all about the mortal confinement into which I had gotten myself. Then again, the mortal side of me did not. I felt upon a hundred occasions that I was "older" than my parents and wanted to convey how wrong and narrow they seemed to me in many of their pronouncements. It may be argued that every child does likewise. That too I concede. But I want to know why. If children—as maintained by orthodox philosophy—are the physical products of parental procreation, whence arise their impulses to exasperation when the hapless offspring is forced to submit to the dictates of adults, especially when unreasonable? Understand me, I do not refer to antagonisms to normal discipline required to protect and train a child and prepare it for maturity. I refer to exasperations toward parental limitations, the expression of ethical tenets if you please, with which the youngster disagrees.

It took me thirty eight years to find the answer to that mystery. But I found it. It came as the aftermath of a single night's esoteric experience high in the mountains of distant California—when The Door to Revelation opened for me suddenly—that has been concretely and specifically responsible for what I have done in the United States since. But back there in 1893 my father had never heard of esoterics. My parents knew nothing of any aspects of life but those which offered them food and clothing, made them conform to current social dictates and impressed upon them that the Age of Miracles closed nineteen hundred years bygone—when our Lord took a sort of celestial levitation to heavenly realms, thereafter to become divine counsel for the defense, leaving the earth to run itself and talk about His visit through all future time.

In short, they were devout, clean living, orthodox people, strictly circumscribed by the Puritanic code of ethics and a literal interpretation of the Jewish Holy Scriptures. And born unto them had been a small, tow-headed cub who occasionally said or did things that brought qualms about his sanity. My zeal for entering anything which lured me had a maturity that caused much consternation. I speak of certain incidents, I say again, to proclaim not my precocity but because I believe that in my own case I was proving something that my father's fundamentalism had tragically passed by. This again concerns the opening of the Door. I read fluently before I started school. I startled my parents of a week in 1895 when they opened their copy of the weekly Zion's Herald and beheld a contribution in The Youth's Letter-Box signed William Dudley Pelley. I had written and mailed the letter myself. It attested to the large experience of myself as gardener, containing among other assertions which required a certain editing, " . . . I have had beans spring up on me in one night." This was accurately the first time anywhere that the name of this author appeared publicly in print. Thereafter the stamp box was kept beyond my reach. . . .

Again to forecast the Opening of the Door, I cannot remember a time when a public rostrum has not seemed as familiar to me as my chair at a table or a stool before a type case. I say that something was "poking through" in those years, to be propounded later on. I was no child prodigy. Such things as prodigies, correctly understood, I declare do not exist. Quite another process is at work, as I dramatically found out. But neither father, mother, nor myself knew it at the time.

The other day I passed the house into which we moved when mother and I took a motor trip for a day to East Templeton. It stands on the south side of the highway, halfway up the first grade running westward from the village, a little flat box-house with barn adjoining. How small and tawdry and barren it looked! How big and well kept and bowered in trees and shrubs it once was, as I had remembered it throughout four decades of absence!

Father bought this little house and a score of acres of land about, colloquially known as the Fairbanks Place, early in 1895, and there we made our residence for the ensuing two years. During this time a sainted soul whom I knew as Grandma Fairbanks gave me my first instruction in reading, using her sewing shears to point out the words in a book of Aesop's Fables. She had reserved two of the upstairs rooms for occupancy until her death as a condition of the sale.

She was a patient-faced New England grandmother who wore her hair behind in a tight little walnut and only ventured forth into the village on a Sabbath morning when she put on a rusty bonnet, draped a genuine Paisley shawl about her rotund figure and attended divine service in the same church in which I had once held forth to my father's consternation. Those all-too-brief years in East Templeton when we lived "downstairs under Grandma Fairbanks" remain in my memory as the perfect idyll of New England existence. When many years later I filled the fiction magazines of the country with homely stories of "Paris, Vermont" and the adventures of Sam Hod and his partner in conducting The Paris Daily Telegraph, it was this Massachusetts village of East Templeton that I called to do service as my "Foxboro Center, just over the mountain." .. .

Certain items stand out in recollection poignantly: the aforementioned death of Carrie while we lived in this house, my first sight of an electric car when the railway came through from Gardner, the sweet piping of spring frogs in the wallow down below the pasture, the dank smell of the rushes that grew along the Causeway where the road from the village bisected twin ponds, church bells tolling beautifully on summer Sabbath mornings, my mother's clear but slightly melancholy voice singing hymns in opal twilight, or the jingle of the bells on sleighs and bobsleds in the icy winter as they mounted the hill before the house and up into carmine sunset. No hurtling Sunday motorists disturbed the calm of that New England ruralism. I wandered the surrounding country by summer and winter, got into many of the scrapes depicted in The Fog, my second novel, finally approached that fraught period when I must start to school. But before doing so, I underwent another queer experience that lifted the Veil thus early on the Life-Behind-Life... .

One singing summer morning, with Edna an infant in her cradle and my elders busy elsewhere, I went out behind the house. The apple blossoms were heavy on the gnarled trees about me. A small knoll lifted south eastward at the edge of the mowing. I halted on this knoll and surveyed the bright landscape.

I looked at piled clouds in the beryline sky. I looked across meadow, pasture and woodlot. I watched bevies of butterflies warbling into distance. At length I looked down—almost at my feet. An ant ran up a grass stalk, found no further place to go, and descended as it came. All the world was lush with life. The universe throbbed with it. Then

114

with a sense of shock, my attention came to rest on the body that I occupied. It was a healthy but dumpy little body. The feet were quite grimy. I believe one toe was wrapped in a rag. Despite my five years, I suddenly asked myself a question from the depths of Ageless Wisdom:

How had I come into that little boy's body? What was I doing in it indeed, in this vibrant world that deployed all about me? What if all of it had never "happened"? Where would I be then? I knew I would be somewhere.

It seemed as though, for an instant, standing on that knoll, a corner of the veil of Eternal Mortality was flashingly lifted, that despite all the assurance of my father's theology, I had known such Singing Nature a thousand times before. How funny to be encased in that pudgy little hulk of peregrinating protoplasm that got dirty so quickly, that had to be fed and washed and put to bed nightly, whose nether portions could be spanked with such blighting embarrassment! Where had all of these human beings come from? Where had the ant come from that ran up the stalk? Where had father and mother come from, and my "new" sister Edna? Yes, and where had Carrie, my playmate of yesteryear, "gone"?

I knew. I knew! It came to me for a fleeting instant on that meadow upland. Then immortality shut down. I was the minister-cobbler's small son again. And two months later found me in school... .

During my first two years of schooling I got my first notions of national politics. Bryan made his celebrated Cross of Gold speech at the Chicago convention and gangs of boys went to and fro in the schoolyard demanding of me—and others—whether we were Republicans or whether we were Democrats. I appealed to my father...

"Pa, am I a Republican or a Demmy-crack?"

"Why," he responded, "you're a Republican."

"Why am I a Republican?"

"Because I'm a Republican—and you happen to be my son."

Thus I discovered that politics had much in common with religion—or for that matter, citizenship itself. You are born into all of them.

I reported to my schoolmates that I "stood" for McKinley. "All right," they decided. And forthwith I was exempt from manhandling—or maybe it was boy-handling—and joined in mussing up such other boys as had Demmy-crack fathers...

Two autumns, two winters, and two springtimes, I went to that village school. I knew how a half-frozen lunch tasted from a pail that smelled of the grease of many homemade doughnuts. I experienced the horror of Friday afternoon "piece speakin' " when the selectmen came in to take note of our eloquence. I idled on my way home from school, summer and winter, as boys will idle. I knew the joys of entering a warm house in the twilight, with only an oil lamp burning in the kitchen but the odor of frying potatoes savory from the stove. After supper I had my chores to do, and split my morning kindling. Another world, all of it, where life was wholesome and not an alien nightmare! From the first day that I set foot in The Gardner Journal office there was something hauntingly familiar about it. Not that particular office... any printing office. No one had to show me how to hold a "stick" properly. I seemed to know the type printer's case by instinct—only it wasn't instinct. Every moment of my spare time, after we moved to Gardner,

I spent about those premises. Snatching up any composing stick that a compositor laid down, I made for a stool and set up lines of type. I remember Old Man Whitaker, one of the paper's proprietors, exclaiming at the way I quadded out my lines. "Who taught you to do that?" he demanded, astonished.

I looked at him in equal wonder. Why should anyone "teach" me how to do it? It was simply done that way, and what more could be said? "Oh, I learnt it years ago," I cried disdainfully... this at the ripe old age of seven.

The fascination which presses, type, and the smell that inked paper held for me became my boyhood's dominant note. When irate compositors finally escorted me from the premises none too gently because they always found my name set up in precisely that composing stick which they required to use next, the burning ambition of my small life was to have my own office and work my own outfit. One of the bitter disillusions of my childhood carne from answering an advertisement in a Sunday supplement that offered "a complete printing outfit" to any juvenile who mailed one dollar to the advertisers. To get that dollar I ran my legs off on errands, conducted a lemonade stand, sold papers on the streets. Had the price been ten thousand dollars it would have seemed no larger nor harder to secure. All the same, I got it. I took four silver quarters to father, asking him to see that they were properly mailed. For a week I dozed to sleep each night envisioning equipment presently to arrive which in a later generation should have been capable of printing The Saturday Evening Post. I prepared a room in the cellar, estimated where I meant to locate the press, where the type racks and imposing-stones should stand. Finally the express man tossed out a package addressed to me, not much larger than a good-sized cigar box. I cut the strings, puzzled, wondering who had sent me a gift out of season. Thereupon I lifted out a dinky little contraption of cheapest cast iron about the size of a corporation's seal. In the box was a little tray of types, each one thrust down endways, two characters only to each compartment. There was likewise an ink dauber and a little tube of ink. In cold horror I looked at the manufacturer's name upon the wrapper and grasped that here at last was my printing plant. . . . There were not enough types to set up my name.

I fled blindly to the cellar and wept bitter tears. That dollar had come hard. While father was not exactly calloused, this denouement caused him laughter. "You'll learn by such experiences," he told me, "never to buy a pig in a bag."

"But I didn't want a pig. I wanted a printing plant like Whiting & Whitaker's."

"Did you actually think you could get such a plant for one dollar? The newspaper said a printing outfit. I'm sorry, son. But let this be a lesson never to give up money for anything without seeing first just what you're buying."

The Oak Street district in the northwest part of town has long since been built up into a smart suburban neighborhood. But in those bygone days of the Spanish War it was almost "in the country" . . . the woods came down from Bancroft's Hill nearly to our rear door. With Willie Leamy, a boyhood chum, I tramped those woods. We came to know every square foot of that sylvan paradise. We knew every bypath, every pine glade, every swampland, every bog-hole. We knew where to look for the first trailing arbutus, and where the lady's slippers grew in the warmth of piny hillsides. We knew where to go to scare out the partridges. We knew how to locate the haunted spot that had seen the death of a hunting youth by the accidental discharge of the rifle of a friend. No boy who has not known his New England--or American— woodlands between six and ten years old, has the proper experience to ballast his life.

I lived those far-off years in the very heart and essence of a clean, wholesome, untarnished America which must be brought back. Each year held four holidays sacredly observed in the best Nordic tradition: Memorial Day, Independence Day, Thanksgiving and Christmas. Those were the years when the Grand Army of the Republic was still a power in the land, and the decorating of the graves of soldiers who had died for the Union was a hallowed obligation. Never do I smell the fragrance of moist lilacs in the springtime that I am not carried back to those Memorial Days when hosts of men in blue, the silver beginning to show in their hair, placed New England flowers tenderly on mossy mounds beneath which comrades of other years were sleeping.

When July 4th arrived, we boys got up before dawn and made the air hideous with blastings and boomings. We shot off our firecrackers, we shot off our cannon, we shot off our fingers. What mattered it? Our forebears at Monmouth, Lundy's Lane, and Gettysburg, had lost their arms, their legs, and withal their lives.

And the same thing went for Thanksgiving. We had the story of the Pilgrim Fathers and the Mayflower Compact. We could recite "The breaking waves dashed high on a stern and rockbound coast" till the ghost of old Chief Massasoit strode right into our classrooms. The next day for the epochal meal of the year at home, we had turkey and cranberry sauce—the only day of the year when we did have it. Thanksgiving was thanks giving. It was good to live in those days and know such a heritage. What red-blooded man would not exert himself to the utmost to see that they are brought back?

My Christmases were distinguished by the unfailing arrival of my mother's affluent sister, Georgia, from her home in Peabody. Aunt Georgia was conceded to have made the best matrimonial match in the Goodale family of daughters, in that she had wedded the scion of a wealthy leathern-goods manufacturer. She had been twice to Europe and withal was childless—not that going to Europe could have had much to do with making her otherwise. So days before Christmas she made it an annual rite to hunt the Boston stores with a well-filled pocketbook—not known to sisters who had merely married ministers— and at length packed a crate of the latest toys and candies to make our Yuletide memorable. On the day before Christmas came the lady in person—the only day in the year when the depot hack drove up to our house. Her silk skirts swished in the best Gay Nineties manner and she was fragrant with perfume. She wore fearful and wonderful hats and had gold in her teeth. Her prize distinction in my eyes was a unique watch which had neither numerals nor hands upon its face but told the time by the sudden appearance of the exact hour and moment within little compartments in the center of the dial.

Once she was housed in the "company" bedroom, the unpacking of her boxes and parcels began. We brought in and set up the Christmas tree, selected months before in Bancroft's woods. My Grandmother Goodale-Thurston was infallibly present. Whereupon we made merry in another tradition, quite as patriotic as it is American and Christian. For once in the year I had all the candy I could gorge. The house on Christmas morning, with all of Aunt Georgia's latest toys and gifts, was the sort of place that little children dream about, no matter how much silver has come into their hair. What Christmas in my boyhood would have been without my wealthy Aunt Georgia is hard to conjecture.

I was hoarding my savings to get myself a real printing press. With laudable parental wisdom in raising a small son and making him appreciate the value of his possessions by paying for them in labor, he offered me two cents a bundle for every delivery on my bicycle. Furthermore, he leaned toward no indulgences in the items that he gave me to deliver. I pedaled about Springfield for the next three years on an oversized "wheel," leaving everything at the front doors of citizens from sacks of fertilizer to Easter lilies. I had a wire gadget attached to my handlebars. I would pile this with bundles till I could scarcely see above them.

One night, after the day's deliveries, father met me at home with the epochal announcement, "The Kidder Printing Company up on Bay

Street has a practical hand press that I think you could use. We'll drive over after supper and see if it suits."

Eat my supper with a press in sight at last? But I swallowed plenty when we got to Bay Street and discovered that the owners of the shop wanted twenty dollars for the press whereas my savings were but twelve. Father saw my nausea.

"I'll loan you what you're short," he offered, "providing you'll continue to work it out in bundle deliveries."

It was a compact, substantial hand press that took a form six inches by nine. It weighed so much that two men had to carry it out to the wagon. I rode home sitting beside it as interns accompany patients to hospitals in ambulances. I had a shop all ready for it in a small room off the stable. We had moved from 17 Spruce Street to 132 Florence Street during the interval that I saved the twelve dollars and the barn out behind was well suited to my purpose. I had been collecting printing-supply catalogues and haunting Springfield's printing offices for odds and ends of fixtures. One day behind The Springfield Printing & Binding Company I found a discarded spill of reglet thrown out in the alley. It resembled the sort of dream that some of us have, of coming upon a pile of money scattered over the sidewalk. I salvaged it and sorted it. I made tables and type racks from pieces of lumber. My first imposing stone was a slab of marble taken from the bathroom of an abandoned neighboring house.

Father had ideas about saving himself money on his printing. "You can't run a printing office without type," he informed me. As if I did not know it! "You pick out what you need from the catalogues and I'll finance the payment. If you take in a job printing you can pay me back exactly like a bank."

I would have contracted to tote a Jersey cow to the top of the Springfield Arsenal and hang overside by her tail if it got me that equipment. I ordered a dozen fonts of type and enough eight-point to fill a chase with text. At last I was a printer! So at the tender age of twelve I started a journal that I called The Junior Star.

Several issues of The Star had been handed about the schoolyard, each of them delayed for publisher's reasons, when I took my seat in the class one noontime with a small green grass snake secreted in my pocket. Ahead of me sat a buxom lass named Hazel. The bulge of Hazel's frock at the back of her neck held a certain fascination, and the particular devil that motivates small boys wrought a swift coordination of enticements and impulses. I took out my entirely harmless little reptile and dropped it down her neck!

If I had dropped a pound of gunpowder into the school's hot furnace, I could not have managed a better explosion. Hazel was out in the aisle in a shake—in fact a great many shakes—frantically clawing the interior of her person. Clothes at the moment were anathema on principle. And she started a screeching that aroused the whole building.

Now my teacher of the period was a lady of some temperament who had failed to catch a man. But if she had failed to catch a man, she showed every indication of success in catching a plump and screeching girl and making her reveal the cause of her contortions. Somehow the snake dropped out and wriggled down a floor-crack. The teacher knew this thing had happened because girls in that classroom climbed high on their desks. That was about the time that I decided, regardless of the hour, that I should leave and go home. But the woman nabbed me going. The principal was sent for. He was a doughty Civil War veteran with a hand like a blackjack.

Somehow I talked myself out of that scrape. Arriving at home and in the silence of my print shop, I decided however I did not like that teacher—she was totally devoid of the slightest sense of humor, or what passes for humor in the philosophy of boys. I decided, in short, that something was wrong with the whole public school system when such humorless females were placed in jurisdiction over up-and-coming youngsters. I would write the woman up and expose her in my paper.

I did write the woman up and expose her in my paper. Had I kept to an attack on the public school system, it would not have been so bad. But I had acquired sundry copies of Elbert Hubbard's Philistine and the sage of East Aurora had become my patron saint. I was steeped in the sweet vitriol of the erstwhile Fra Elbertus and I used it on my pen. I particularly emphasized that teacher's spinster status and told my reasons for it from a six-month observation. I gave my own account of the snake episode as though the whole world were waiting to receive it. The paper was printed. It offered comments on the gapes in Hazel's clothing and said that if I had to be chastised for the hapless business, it was a pity that the teacher's clothing had not received the reptile, it seemed to bulge everywhere ….remarks of that tenor.

Nothing I have ever published about the activities of America's radicals in the past five years has created one-half the denouement that resulted when someone laid a copy on the aforesaid teacher's desk. She dismissed school early. She got her hat. She likewise got her umbrella—or perhaps it was her parasol. Straight for my parental domicile she smoked. She bothered to take along no small boy as

Exhibit A in all the brilliant business; she probably thought she could lay hands on him at any time she wanted. Her one-track mind at the moment was prompting her to interview the parents who had been so brash as to give a small boy the uncensored use of a printing press and types. I skirted fourteen blocks in order to arrive at home that evening. When I finally summoned up the courage to go in, the woman was just leaving. Both she and my father had significant gleamings in their eyes. Mother was wisely keeping her silence.

"Well, young man?" my father demanded.

"Yes, sir," I said carelessly, assuming an innocence.

"It seems that you've got me into a rather ugly mess. Don't you know there are some things you can't print in a paper without running the risk of being sued for libel?"

"What's libel?" I faltered.

"Printing the truth about people—too truthfully."

"Then what is it called when you happen to print lies?"

"We won't discuss the political phases of the situation. Now what's this mess about?"

I tried to tell him.

"Ho-hum," he ruminated. His face held a queer look. "Perhaps you'll get along."

I usually had an instinct when father was going to larrup me. These symptoms seemed lacking. I heard him continue ….

"I think you'd better change the name of your paper and sort of confine it to literary subjects. As for what you've done today ....well, you'll learn in militant journalism that whatever you print is just about as safe from reprisal as your opponent's secret dread of you. You've said some unkind and impudent things about your teacher. She's been over here saying a lot of worse things about me for ever turning you loose with a printing press. But I don't have to take the press away from you. You've got to go to school to that woman for the balance of this year. Don't come whining to me if the going gets too tough."

I crept into classroom next morning desperately hoping that I would not be noticed. No such good luck. That teacher noticed no other child that day. Yet the day held surprises. She greeted me with a pleasant good-morning and in forenoon recitation she gave me all the breaks. The week and the month wore scholastically onward. She was so increasingly saccharine in her treatment of me that I began to be troubled. The other boys were seeing it—with schoolyard reprisals. All of it was coals of fire upon my youthful head. Almost a year had passed and I was about to move along into high school before the correct explanation got through my brain.

The woman was afraid that I might lampoon her again!

I confess to my guilt from the beginning of the incident. That teacher had every license to truss me by the thumbs from the rafters and flay me. But she could not afford to have more infant drivel distributed over Springfield to the hazard of her job. She was so nice to me that it began to dawn upon me how Voltaire might have felt when he wrote, "I may not possess a scepter but I do possess a pen!"

I give my father credit for being wise enough to know that tanning my seat for what I had done, or denying me my printing outfit, would have put a dangerous complex into my journalistic courage. Being wise as a newspaperman himself, he knew that sooner or later I would encounter my own reprisals from over-indiscretions. It was a sage thing to do.

In February of that year father came home one night bringing the stupefying announcement that he had sold his delivery business. Moreover the price he had received was sizable enough to start him manufacturing with a partner named Sibley. This Sibley had invented an improved tissue-paper winder for toilet rolls—or convinced father that he had—which would revolutionize the business. Father was going out to York State with Sibley and in due time we would hear from him. He went, and we did.

He came back to drop a second bombshell directly in the center of the Pelley ménage. He was taking me out of school!

Yes, my education, academically, was finished. No college for me, nor high school graduation. It was my duty to accompany him to York State and help him make his millions via rolled-up tissue paper.

The prospect appalled me. I did not want to stop my schooling. I was then a sophomore at Technical High, the publisher of a more pretentious and successful monthly magazine called The Black Crow, president of the high school debating society, and standing so high in my English course that I never was required to take semi-annual exams. What could I do in a mill, making paper?

All of it was futile, my bitter remonstrance. The night we left for Fulton, a city north of Syracuse, a zero blizzard stopped us at Schenectady. The two of us put up at a small, cheap hotel. I remember my tears throughout most of that night. I wanted to go onward and complete my education, go to college, become an editor, an author.

"No," said father. "Paper!"

Now I appreciate that it was part of my role to have that invaluable experience in manufacturing, to learn business fundamentals through hard and grueling practice, to know the problems of the employer, to learn to handle men. My writing would come later. And most certainly it did. That wintry night in Schenectady, however, with the icy blasts rattling the casements and the room over-hot from a surcharge of steam, I found myself venomously critical of my father for what I considered his parental despotism over my destiny. What right had he to ruin my prospects and subvert my talents because he needed the aid of his son in his business? When we finally reached Fulton and I perceived that the much-vaunted factory was but a forty-foot room in which worked one sluttish girl and a small boy with adenoids, my disillusion was complete.

In all of this, father was but an instrument at the command of higher forces. I believe it now—visualizing that sequence in perspective—with absolute conviction. I have shocked a good many people from time to time, telling them to stop their sniveling at what they imagine their parents have done to them. Weird as it may sound, to those hearing this sort of thing for the first time, I have the same adamant conviction that we actually choose our parents, of our own free will, before entering life as infants. We know in advance, before we are physically born, I say, what the factors and trends in a given life will be ...by selecting certain parents. The choice is our own. They merely prepare the embryo of which we take possession. We either want what they have to give us, or we do not. We may not always know it in our conscious minds, but eventually it will come to us.

But I did not recognize this great grim principle of esoterics at the time of which I write. Like a hundred million mortals who may not as yet have had the Door to Revelation opened to them, who, in consequence, fancy themselves defeated and thwarted, I accepted the silly tenets of orthodoxy that I had been assembled and projected into life by parental procreation, that fate had decreed me to serve a 21-year sentence to their caprices and tempers, to be finally discharged with my future a mess. What a hodge-podge of blither! As if the physical acts of a man or woman could ever concoct an immortal soul capable of writing a book or exclaiming at a sunset. But what was worse in my case, I beheld in those parents all adulthood in conspiracy against my spiritual integrity, with a smug God looking on woodenly and giving the scheme His blessing. In fact, my father reminded me that God was on his side—and I think that he believed it.

Father was really a sincere but inhibited man who had a hard row to hoe but who finally hoed it, to whom I owe the eternal debt of a sound and normal body, the sturdy tenets of morality derived from a theology that stood for no monkey-business, and last but far from least, an inspirational philosophy that urged me to make the most of myself no matter what sacrifice was entailed in the process. He was harsh with the harshness of limited vision, but he did the best he knew according to his light. His religion frowned on drinking, dancing, card-playing, theater-going. During the days of the parcel delivery our only recreation aside from divine service on Sundays was attending a series of Sabbath afternoon lectures sponsored by the Springfield Young Men's Christian Association in Court Square Theater, which the foremost public men of America addressed. I had the profit of their counsel and ideals from the platform and father and I scarcely missed a one of them. Statesmen, publicists, economists, scientists, explorers …that contact with them was priceless, not for what they said but for what they represented. Henry Cabot Lodge, S. S. McClure, Senators Dolliver, Beveridge, and LaFollette, William Jennings Bryan, Governor Curtis Guild, Sir William Grenfel . . . these men dramatized ideals.

On many a homeward walk after those meetings, father would put his arm about my shoulders and adjure me: "No matter what becomes of me, son, or in what situation you later find yourself, make the most of your life —NEVER LET IT GET YOU DOWN!"

Would to God that the boys of our present generation could live beneath such influences, in such years as I knew them.

But back there in Fulton in 1907, with academic education definitely behind me, I was a resentful young cub, certain that my sire was both bigoted and selfish. Did he propose to force me into being an adult ahead of my time? Very well, I would show him. If I had to smother and repress my literary talents, go to work at the blast of a whistle every morning, then insanely I demanded a grown man's prerogatives. Of course the chief of these is Woman. I began to look at Woman as I had not observed her. I made it my business to fall violently in love!

Naturally a certain diffidence maintains when a man turns his pen to the affairs of his heart. The intimacies of his spirit, about which his patrons would like to know most, turn to inhibitions controlled by sacrosanct urgings, that dictates of good taste take into account the relationships involving others. But there were significant factors in that first love affair of mine that belong to this saga from the literary standpoint.

It is sufficient to state that the young woman's name was Mabel and that she was a Canadian lass who came down to Fulton to visit an aunt and uncle for the winter. I met her in the choir of the Methodist Church—which father joined at once—where she sang a sweet soprano, and I also made noises in a supposedly sacred manner. I looked upon her, and she looked upon me, and presently we transferred our noise making to her uncle's front parlor …where it ceased to be sacred. I found pleasure in bellowing out the popular ballads of the day while she furnished the proper piano accompaniment.

This sort of thing began one night a week at first, then twice in every week, then six nights in the week. Whereupon, having been forced into the life of a man insofar as business duties and payrolls were concerned, and scarcely understanding the primordial shudders that went through my person as I cuddled her close beneath an April umbrella, I saw nothing inconsistent in wanting my precocious maturity rounded out by the addition of a helpmate.

131

Just why I needed a mate, and at what she was to help, I paused to give no thought. The girl had a piquant nose, a well-matured bosom, a capricious ankle and a flare for toothsome cookery. She banged the parlor's musical equipment with quite as much cooperation as I put into yowling Charles K. Harris' tuneful banalities. In a matter of weeks we had parish tongues wagging. We were seen walking together in places of solitude at unseasonable hours. The girl came back from such excursions with her hair out of pin and when she was queried, her manner was saucy. Thirty years ago it savored of Ruin!

Father came alive." What, What? Matrimony? At my age?"

He looked at me as though I had strangled my grandmother. Mother was present and put her portion over. Parental fiats made an end to the session. Father vowed that he would smash the infamous business if he had to break my neck …whereupon he broke plenty, but my neck was not included. He was not particularly delicate in the manner of his breaking.

When another week had passed and the news was cudgeled out of me that I had twice seen Miss Mabel, he took me to my chamber. He threatened me, he cuffed me, he even went so far as to lock me in that bedroom while he deployed across the town and took the matter up with the young woman's relatives. I lifted the sash and went down the rainspout. Beating father to her home by a matter of moments, I whistled my lady-love down from her premises. We walked far afield discussing the denouement.

The spring night was freighted with the incense of lilacs. After a time, the moon arose and joined us. We stayed out so late that even the frogs ceased piping in soft distance. But we came to no decision. What was there to decide? I lacked three years of reaching my majority. I was wholly dependent on my father for my living. A shotgun wedding? No—we did not go in for that sort of thing. Our generation had raised us differently.

It was one of the most poignant evenings which I have ever lived. We had to go back. At the edge of town the girl stopped beneath a wild cherry tree in blossom. She broke off a sprig and put it in her hair. Near the steps to the house she handed it to me. I kept the poor fragile little thing for years—till at last it fell apart.

Eschewing companionships that were pale echoes of my romance, I gave thought to my schooling which the mill had interrupted. Gradually it dawned on me that even academics were not confined to classrooms. If I wanted education, what prevented me from taking it? The lore of the world was contained in its books. I had but to read and all knowledge was my heritage.

I did read. I drugged myself with reading. I read long, serious books, curiously enough mostly history and biography. I wanted to know how other men had solved problems much like mine, how they had met crises, whether I was peculiar in my reactions to my parents. For twenty five years I have read myself to sleep in bed every night.

One night I walked into the newspaper's proof room. I found there a buxom young woman who was softly sympathetic regarding my recent business losses [due to short-sighted decisions by a new board of directors]. I submitted written drivel for her to approve. She not only approved it, but she offered prescriptions for my temperamental lassitude. What I truly needed was a vacation, she said. And what better place to take it than in southern Vermont at the home of her parents?

The spring of 1911 found me out of a job. The prospect of vacation struck me as unique. I had just had three months while my business went to rack. But perhaps the girl was right. I could play around now without worries to rend me. She seemed a good pal to even suggest it. Would she go up with me? She said that she might. . . . A few weeks later, in the kitchen of an old Vermont farmhouse, with sweet summer rain pattering on the shingles, I asked if she would marry me. She said that she might. . . .

NEWSPAPER MAN, WAR CORRESPONDENT

After the Door opened for me, in 1928, many professional psychologists took a morbid relish in analyzing my case—from fragmentary biographies—and informing the public from their asinine profundities that all that prompted the more dramatic episodes of my life was exaggerated neurasthenia. Now neurasthenia, according to the best dictionaries, is brain and nerve exhaustion, a depression of the vital forces. Lengthy monographs have from time to time been published explaining in much detail my addictions to such exhaustions and depressions, principally penned of course by persons who never have met me in their lives.

One expert paid me the doubtful compliment of calling me a Shattered Soul. I say "paid me a compliment" because I have uniformly found that the easiest way for experts to rationalize the behavior of a person who seeks to do anything out of the ordinary is to call his soul "shattered". Most analyses of the outstanding men of this or past generations have proven them shattered souls—beyond the fraction of a doubt. It is truly amazing what these personages of history accomplished as soon as their souls became properly shattered.

But let an infant kick the slats from its cradle in rebellion at the temperature of its milk, show signs of precocity in adolescence, affront the dictates of the social herd in early maturity, and generally bother God and the angels with expositions of his own individuality when he reaches those years when he can do something about it besides lament it, and it is demonstrated beyond the peradventure of a challenge that life has kicked his soul in the face and shattered the poor thing into fifty seven pieces.

To all of it, fiddlesticks!

I never have had much use for people who let the commonplaces of existence keep them commonplace, anyhow. I have had still less use for men and women who live their lives scared to death that perchance by giving free vent to their inner urges they may actually accomplish something that will leave them marooned on a social island of rugged individualism. I like people who are first and foremost themselves. When a man lives sincerely, without artifice or timidity, I know what he is and just where to find him when I need the particular brand of personality or intellectual or moral attainments that he has to contribute. It's far better to be eccentric when it is artless eccentricity than to be the most erudite rascal with a flawless conformity.

Some people slide into life to awaken in physical bodies with silver cutlery thrusting from their mouths. They have pleasant, carefree childhoods. They scarcely know a care or a worry, even up to marriage. When they mate off, they still pursue a fairly even tenor of existence, give birth to their progeny, make a comfortable living, belong to all the best clubs and lodges, and then distinguish themselves by dying in sacrosanct decorum. The cemeteries of the world are stuffed with the husks of such mediocrities who had no special errands to consummate excepting to themselves.

No worlds have taken fire in that they existed. They have been the great rank-and-file who sometimes have committed suicide when financial reverses were so ungracious as to touch them, or perished of broken hearts when their mates have eloped with stenographers or icemen. There are other people who have come into life to make a great dent on society's moral apathy, to shake up the cycles wherein they perform, to function as pioneering spirits in political, economic, or martial upheavals—or perhaps to write only one poem, or paint one picture, that influences the culture of a nation or a race. They know it all before hand but temporarily forget it when mortality snugs about them. To do that job well, they ask for the bitterest possible doses of mortal vicissitude. They want life to take them by the scruff of the neck and rub their noses, from the cradle to the grave, in the abrasive gravels of trenchant experience. They ask for this sort of thing ...and get it.

They get it, I believe, by deliberately choosing the types of parents through whom they shall be born, or the known environment in which those parents raise them. They begin to acquire worldly experiencing with the casting off of pinafores. They find themselves batted around, maltreated and generally suppressed. When they come to maturity, they take their romances with lightning-bolt severity. If a woman or two lets them down, it is done by a sort of preconceived arrangement that such are their roles, to deliver the victims ...who are not at all victims ...their several doses of grueling heartbreak making for increment in spiritual balance.

We had been married on December 16, 1911, by the Rev. A. D. Chadsey. Harriet, our first daughter, was born the next year. Thereupon I knew all the throes of being the proud and finicky young father. But long before that happened I came to the conclusion that I could not work for wages. It was anathema to my temperament. Although without funds, I promoted a newspaper. I had to promote it.

The wife I had married was Marion Harriet Stone and she had been horn in Millers Falls, MA of a mother who was a Waste. The Wastes are too well known in northwestern Massachusetts for me to eulogize them here. The name, I was told, was a derivative from West, and the Wests from whom they in turn were derived were the equally well-known clan that signed the Mayflower Compact.

We were mated intellectually, and in a manner of speaking, professionally—she having followed the printing craft like myself on finishing school, learning her business of proofreading at the Cambridge plant of Houghton, Mifflin & Co. Temperamentally, however, we were as opposite as the poles. I was creative, venturesome, crusading. Life to me was a constant campaign with objectives to be won and heights to be conquered. Marion was conservative even to complacency. She viewed life, it later seemed to me, not as a campaign but rather as a program. You lived life, not in reaction to a Pounding Urge that banged your chassis to pieces if you could not get traction, but by arising at seven o'clock each morning and having your breakfast. Then you repaired to your daily labors and pursued them diligently until it was time to go home at night—with an hour off for lunch. You did this six days a week, with the Sabbath off for rest, four weeks to the month, twelve months to the year. At the end of each year you were one year older, just as at the end of each week, and you were certain dollars richer. You used this money to pay the bills incurred by living, and if you could contrive a surplus, you banked it. Gradually you got ahead and owned a little better and larger homestead, and had a larger circle of more affluent friends. When you finally came to die, the local newspaper said nice things about you—perhaps half a column—and all sorts of people attended your funeral.

Such was living life "successfully" as it was held up to me. I have no comment to make upon it, excepting that for some people it may be commendable and suitable ....but that I am not one of them! To me, that sort of existence was a kind of paralysis. It was walking about in a state of living death. Each day to me was a challenge to achieve, to essay something more noteworthy or impelling in character than yesterday or last week. Each day was a separate life-cycle unto itself, with its beginning and its ending, its inception and its climax. To do the same thing twice in succession, in the same manner and at the same tempo, was to demonstrate that nothing had been learned, that no progress had been made, that the spirit had gone static.

After that unbelievable catastrophe at the factory, too, when my most sensitive years at industrial effort had culminated in financial fiasco, I was left with a fixation in regard to money that from Marion's standpoint was as abstruse as it was hapless. Money to me was a means to an end. For a matter of years I had ruthlessly conserved and compounded money. When it got into the hundred thousand dollar status, the unstable and ephemeral nature of Money had suddenly revealed itself. As an intrinsic value within itself, it was data on books. If the figures were sizable enough, you wrote checks against them and had delivered what you wanted. Somehow it was a false standard by which to measure achievement, since you had it one moment in sizable quantities, or your bank teller told you that you did, and the next moment, through no particular fault of your own, you did not. Millions of my industrious and thrifty fellow citizens have come through this Depression with their standards of money similarly altered. Only I had such adjustment at the time of my majority. Money had proved a false friend, quite as much as it had been a Frankenstein, at the crisis in our business. It left me with a strange complex in regard to Money that it only became of importance when I did not possess enough of it for some project in hand.

This became utterly incomprehensible to the girl I had married. I have no word of criticism to offer on her philosophy. Femininity's first demand on life is Security. This is particularly true if the woman be maternal. Her children must be provided for in order to nurture them for their places in society. Marion did not see life in terms of any particular dragons to be vanquished, unless they were the dragons of one's personal improvidence. She was fiercely maternal, almost fanatical about the welfare and the safety of her children as they were born. Still, we had obligations and responsibilities of a cosmic nature toward each other that had to be discharged. And we proceeded to discharge them.

There was always a bit of the little Newfoundland lad in father that was altogether lovable. He wanted to show his easy ability to cope with life as he found it down here in "the States", and when things went against him, his blue eyes showed panic. One day he came to me and half-ashamedly wanted to borrow the money to go to New York and take a job with a paper house. I was glad to let him have it. I contemplated transferring the scene of my journalistic endeavors to Vermont and hoped that he could make enough to keep him and mother. The night before I left for Vermont, having taken a job with The Deerfield Valley Times, I bade him goodbye on the side veranda of the Florence Street house where he stretched in the hammock. The soft August evening was vibrant with xylophones of crickets. The fragrance of syringas bathed us as with incense. How could I know we had come to the parting? Strangely enough, in that last hour I spent with him, we talked of religion, of Pastor Russell's Watch Tower Society in which father had found an interest. I finally kissed him and went down the walk to the car line with bags containing combings of my possessions that had been in mother's custody.

I am a grown man myself now and have lived to see my own boy declare his personality, differ from my views, show definite inclinations for living his own life. Perhaps my father learned too from his contact with myself. It could not have been one-sided.

I assumed mother's support after she had exhausted the meager savings and property that had been left in her possession. My sister Edna married presently after an interval of working on my paper up in Vermont. I had my own way to make with a wife, a baby, a mother and subsequently a mother-in-law, who looked to me for their principal sustenance. I set my wits to work. I succeeded in worming my way into the ownership of The Deerfield Valley Times in Wilmington, Vermont...

I got a call from the Hospital about midnight. "You'd better come over first thing in the morning," my wife's tight voice suggested. "The baby's been in coma ever since we got her here."

A heavy snow fell that night. I procured a horse and sleigh from Craft's Livery and started alone for Brattleboro. Ernest and Edna must get out the paper. Driving up Hogback Mountain in cold, sunny forenoon, a sense of what lay ahead seized hold of me. As the horse stumbled onward through sun-refracting snowdrifts, I choked back full sobs.

"Oh God, don't let her die!" I groaned in a different agony than I had known to date. "Not my baby! Not mine!" I had to learn that one does not make bargains with Divine Providence.

"We've lost Harriet," was the way it came—in my mother-in law's brave voice. "We'll be back over home on tomorrow noon's train." The little white casket came over from Brattleboro two days later. Old Man Kidder pulled it down from the station on a hand-sled. We held the funeral in the small front room of our Main Street flat. It brought together all the neighbors and relatives. . . . "I am the resurrection and the life," began the village minister. Marion did not weep. She sat beside me on the divan and her hand found mine in a grip of agony. She had shed all her tears in those hours at the hospital. Harriet had died of cerebral meningitis.

Marion had changed and I could not blame her. Perhaps I too had changed as a result of that Gethsemane. At length the spring of 1914 came beautifully over Vermont's Green Mountains. Harriet was lowered into a little grave in a quiet corner of the cemetery on the hill. Few Sabbath mornings passed that Marion and I did not go up among the ragged asters and sweet white clover and tend that tiny plot of ground where we had buried something that was a fragment of ourselves.

When summer arrived, I found myself so deeply entangled in affairs of The Times, principally from milking my business to pay for

Harriet's illness. I had failed with The Times ...failed miserably. And that too in my wife's home town. We owed every tradesman in the place and I still had ghastly bills in Brattleboro. My own mother was half-crazed by Harriet's passing. To complete the irony of my predicament, a new life [Adelaide] was beating beneath by wife's heart.

What was it that father had so often said to me? ..."Stand up to life, never let it get you down!" Yes, I would stand up to life.

On the last day of July our tenement was vacated. I left for Bennington by train via Greenfield. At noon, while waiting at the junction of the Greenfield station, I bought a copy of The Boston Globe. Emblazoned over the front page were foreign dispatches narrating the assassination of a certain Austrian archduke at Sarajevo. "If Serbia does not apologize, Germany may declare war within forty eight hours", declared the text. I rode up to Bennington apprizing myself of the fraught transpirings three thousand miles eastward.

My stories went out and heartrendingly came back. I was being dunned inhumanly to pay something on those bills in Wilmington and Brattleboro. I once compiled a collection of 175 rejection slips that had come to me before editors no longer sent me rejection slips. Throughout the winter of 1914-1915 I typed away, staving off my creditors, buying new typewriter ribbons and fresh reams of paper. Finally one noontime in December, 1914, I came home to lunch. Four months of the most assiduous effort had not sold a story. But I had shut my emotions to all disappointment. It was a war of attrition between those editors and myself, and I meant to show them that I could last longest. "Look under your plate," advised Marion cryptically.

Beneath it was a salmon-colored envelope with the corner-card of The Popular Magazine, published in New York by Street & Smith. I drew forth the contents, scarcely daring to breathe. A check dropped to the tablecloth. The accompanying letter read:

"We are pleased to accept your story "Spirit of the West" and to tender you herewith our check for $50 in payment. If you have any further stories along this order, we would he glad to read them...."

That fifty dollars was the biggest money that I have ever received for a piece of fiction in my life, not for the amount of the payment but for the fact that I could earn it. Furthermore, it had come in just before Christmas when otherwise our Yuletide had promised to be bleak. Marion took twenty dollars of the money and bought the first suit she had acquired since our marriage. We purchased a stock of inexpensive knick-knacks for the Holbrooks and went over to Jacksonville to spend Christmas with the family.

Months later my trembling fingers plucked up a square envelope with the fraught corner-card of The Saturday Evening Post. I pulled forth the terse letter inside with the inimitable scrawl of George Horace Lorimer. Again it was the fact that I could command such attention that supplied most of my thrill. I was winning, winning! Lorimer had written:

"We are most favorably impressed by your story "Li'l Son of a Gun" and if a payment of $300 will be acceptable we will have a check drawn to your order for that amount. We would like to cut the narrative somewhat but our surgery will be painless."

I finally gave up my job on The Banner. I wanted to be free to travel about, to comb for new material, to write according to my moods. Clate, the lovable old rapscallion, had taken a personal interest in the progress of my expanding recognition. But he was still struggling with my yarn about the oil well. "Say," he cried suddenly, shut in with me one night in the cozy back office, "I can't figure out why the devil you keep turning out stories of the wild and wooly west—as if nothing happened right here in Bennington. Take this office for instance—the drama that's occurred in it, or had fetched into it since nine o'clock this morning. Why don't you write up the local color here at home?"

Forthwith he launched into a poignant incident that had filled half a column in the night's Evening Banner. It struck me with a smash. The man was right! He went on:

"There's a book you ought to read called In Our Town. It's by William Allen White of The Emporia Gazette. It's a book of homely sketches of the same sort of American folks who are passing through The Banner office day after day. I think my copy is up here in this cabinet." He pulled a book out and blew off the dust. "Take that home tonight and read it. Then see what you can do about fitting action-plots to that sort of character-drawing. You'll strike a new note."

I did as he suggested. Page after page of In Our Town moved me to tears. I knew these people. They were ordinary, two-legged humans— loving, hoping, laboring, marrying and dying—living their unwept, un- honored and unsung lives as nobly as they could, representative Americans who displayed their poignant heroisms the clock around with never a thought that they were composing the true saga of our century.

Two weeks later I dropped into Jack Hart's Movie House to see a mother-love film on the screen. A woman had been widowed and left with six boys. The plot of the movie had it that all six had turned out to be scalawags—and yet she carried on. I came from that theater doing some thinking. Why not a story in which the sons of a widowed mother all turned out to be world-famous successes? Would it not hold more drama and more wholesome emotion?

I had lately rented a little office across the street from the theater, which Clate often referred to as the Bennington Short Story Mill. I crossed to this office and snapped on the lights. At nine o'clock I began a story about a woman whose boys were all successes. It was one of those rare narratives that literally wrote itself, drawn from my own experience.

Once in my boyhood, while we had been living in the Spruce Street house, my father had been called to Lynn by the illness of his mother. He had taken me with him. All the rest of my uncles had been similarly summoned though the old lady did not die. That scene in her bedroom, however, I had never forgotten. About her bed were gathered five strapping, full-grown sons—clean, fine men. On the bed stretched the form of a life-spent old woman. From her wasted loins these strong men had sprung. They owed their manhood, their virility, their careers to her. The drama of that tableau were seared on my memory.

Now, I wrote the story, simply, naturally, unaffectedly—as I felt it. When around midnight I came to read through my pages, I realized I did not have to alter a comma. With the emotion of it still gripping me, I found an envelope and stamps. I mailed it to John Siddell of The American Magazine as I passed the post office at midnight. Two days later came a telegram:

COME TO NEW YORK AT ONCE. YOUR "MOTHER STORY" KNOCKOUT. WANT TO DISCUSS YOU DOING SERIES FOR US SIMILAR VEIN.

I went to New York and met John Siddell. I was ushered into the offices of Bert Boyden first, the managing editor. He was a strong but kindly faced fellow with a grim chuckle which put me at ease at once. Presently in came a portly, six-foot Scotchman whose hair gave the impression of a rumpled toupee. He had shrewd blue eyes behind rimless spectacles and the most volatile vocabulary in all my experience. "My gawd!" he cried, walking about and waving his arms. "What a story! WHAT a story! You're either a genius or had a lucky accident. How quick can you furnish me five more just like it?"

"As fast as you can pay for them. And it wasn't any 'lucky accident'."

"I'll pay you two hundred and fifty dollars apiece and jump you fifty dollars a series for every six I take thereafter."

I went back to my hotel and wrote another in similar vein— concerning plain ordinary folk who came and went each day through The Banner office. Sid grabbed for it in equal enthusiasm. Not one in the series did he ever turn back on me. I don't recall ever getting a rejection slip from The American Magazine while he remained its editor. "Their Mother" was published in the September issue of The American and exhausted the edition on the newsstands. That awoke other New York magazine men. Arthur Vance of Pictorial Review took a small-town series. Karl Harriman of The Red Book bought twenty-two in a row.

One night subsequently, after a week's absence, I walked into my home. "I've bought the bankrupt Caledonian", I reported to Marion.

Her mouth acquired a grimness. She said, "Having made a fizzle of two papers already, you'd toss our good story money away on a third?"

"I'm not going to toss good story money anywhere. I'm going to MAKE money just to prove that I can do it."

"You don't have to prove anything. Stick to your writing and let's make us a bank account."

"But," I remonstrated, "pecking at a typewriter week after week is boring me stiff. I want to be in the swim of doing something. I want a problem to tackle and solve. This newspaper project gives me that problem. I'm going to revive it as an evening newspaper—"

"The Caledonian or the problem?"

"I want the experience of running a daily of my own."

"And after you've got it, and it's running nicely?"

"When that moment arrives, I'll probably walk out and leave it flat."

"Yes, I dare say you will."

Through all this petty journalistic stramash, the great war in Europe had been going on, gradually settling into a gory stalemate. I still wrote stories for the national magazines, but no acceptance of a new story now gave me one-half the kick that I received from producing a snappy, profitable evening daily, playing around the forms myself, locking myself into the shop after hours and setting my own editorial features directly on the linotype. During that first six months I doubled the circulation. I moved the plant and duplex from the barn-like structure on Central Avenue hill into tight, compact quarters under Randall & Whitcomb's News Room. I bought two new Intertypes and redressed the paper in the matter of typography. In addition to this office rejuvenation, I bargained for one of the best homes available in the town's residential section, and traded my Saxon Six for the latest and most expensive Hudson Super-Six.

Life was zestful for me, indeed, in those Green Mountain months. Society was still reasonably sane, although propaganda to get the United States into the conflict was being mischievously promoted by enemy agents ensconced behind the scenes in Washington and elsewhere. The fates, however, would not leave me in peace. They had no intention of letting me bog down and marry a small-town evening newspaper. One night two men walked into my composing room.

The first words sent my world into a tailspin. "I've come up from New York to see you," he announced, "to find out if I can persuade you to take a trip around the world."

For a moment I regarded him as though he were a lunatic. Why should anybody, especially a Methodist bishop, offer me a trip around the world unless the deal held fishhooks?

"You're aware, I hope," my caller went on, "of the work of the Methodist Centenary. I'm up here representing Dr. Earl S. Taylor of the Centenary Movement. Dr. Taylor was coming through Colorado recently on a train when he happened to buy an American Magazine containing one of your stories. It affected him so powerfully that he exclaimed, `This fellow Pelley is exactly the chap we should send out into the foreign missionary field on our Centenary survey. If he can write of Oriental conditions as movingly as he's written here about life in Vermont, we'll be doing ourselves a service by giving him the trip and paying his expenses.' So," continued Fisher, "that accounts for my being here."

"B-But," I faltered, "I c-can't afford to t-take a trip around the world."

"No one's asking you to spend your own money. In fact, we'd be prepared to furnish your transportation with, say, five thousand dollars to compensate for your time."

I said, "Where's this money coming from?"

Fisher then outlined the generosity of the Rockefeller Foundation in the matter of the Centenary.

My next question was: "Where must I go?"

"You should sail from San Francisco in a month or six weeks. You should go first to Japan by way of Honolulu. After making a survey of foreign missions in Japan you ought to go up through Korea to North China, then around to India. From India you would return home by way of the Holy Land and Egypt. All the compensation we would ask of you would be that you write honestly, interestingly, and graphically of foreign missions as you find them, of the lives of the missionaries, and just what you think of the work they're accomplishing. The trip will take a year."

Came the day and the hour when I glanced about my perfectly appointed little newspaper plant for the last time, shook hands in farewell with my faithful employees, went out into my Hudson with my wife, my child, my mother, and my mother-in-law loaded aboard amid generous assortments of bags and queer parcels. Not that I was taking all of these with me. But I had found that my sailing date permitted us to cross America by motor car. Mother Holbrook and Adelaide would wait in Los Angeles until our return. My own little mother went along for the ride, to come back by train to her home in Springfield.

I still had a half-interest in my newspaper, money in the bank, forty thousand dollars' worth of paid-up insurance on my life, full expenses for the trip, five thousand dollars in Methodist Church drafts handed me in New York, and in addition to all of these, practically ten thousands dollars in currency that I had received that morning from the two local men who were going to conduct the paper until my return. . .
.

Suddenly, magnificently, I beheld a snow-white cone that seemed exotic cloud. "Fujiyama!" explained the Japan-wise among us.

America, Los Angeles where Adelaide and Mother Holbrook stayed, Vermont, my Evening Caledonian office, Bennington, Wilmington, Chicopee, the Fulton factory, the East Templeton parsonage . . . all these were far, far away in another life when our doughty little vessel steamed slowly up Tokyo Bay toward Yokohama that nineteenth afternoon. The only link that bound me to all that I had ever been was the girl I had married that slushy night in Springfield, surrounded now by a bevy of women friends near the prow of the ship, watching the first valiant sampans tacking across our course. I saw that approach to Japan through the eye of the novelist.

Silver sunshine on cobalt water. Gulls and sampans. A low-lying beach of chalky whiteness flowing past us for an hour on the north as our vessel gradually entered Tokyo Bay. The snow-white cone of Fujiyama fading from the sky. Curdles of black industrial smoke arising above the outlines of incongruous skyscrapers. Then a veer toward the north as land showed straight ahead with the vessels of a hundred nations passing or at anchor. Yokohama's bluffs lifting green behind the city on the left. And always the sampans worming hither and yon, sometimes propelled by leg o' mutton sails, sometimes worried forward by naked brown boatmen plying at rudder oars. Then gradually the rising of the miles of docks from brackish yellow water. Everywhere now the fried-egg flag of Japan—the kerchief of yellow with its orange-pink yoke.

A paper nation, a country of children, a land of exquisite culture, infallible courtesy, perfect law and order, inimitable ethics. In all the time that I spent in Japan, I never saw a street brawl, I saw but one drunken person, I never heard a Japanese baby howling nor, conversely, saw one spanked. Courtesy, docility, stiff and formal graciousness—these I saw met by western vulgarity, boorishness, bombast, all-round insolence. I had not been in the Flowery Kingdom a week before I was ashamed of my people, ashamed of what purported to be my "religion," certainly ashamed of the nature of my errand.

I had come out at the expense of a great American church to investigate and report on the efficacy of foreign missions. What need, forsooth, had the Japanese for our religion? I saw them living the ethics of it, day unto day, amongst and between themselves. I saw them as residents of a country where all the fine, intersocial precepts which we as Christians flaunt so brazenly as the end-and-aim of modern civilization, had become so natural to the Japanese that they were scarcely worthy of comment.

I have not the slightest criticism to offer of missionaries as a caste, a group of earnest, self-sacrificing people who had exiled themselves from homeland and friends to remain out there in the Orient's "darkness" and carry the precepts of the Lowly Galilean unto those who knew Him not. But as for the missionary gesture as a gesture—I was almost minded to use the cruder term "racket"—it began to stack up to me as the most nonsensical, insolent, arrogant program that a distant nation of provincials could connive and inflict upon another in the name of Holy Spirit. In other words, it was purely theological. We were trying to "sell" the Japanese not so much on Christian ethics—because they already possessed and practiced those ethics in a way far advanced over ours—but upon a Theological Hypothesis. In other words, the Vicarious Atonement. And the Japanese could comprehend neither one nor the other. Their minds did not function in complexities of doctrine, all more or less philosophical, or if they did, they saw nothing to get so excited about, as these missionaries perceived with their many sects and creeds. All that fuss and pother, I thought, and the raising of millions of money, and the construction of churches and schools and traveling to and fro on steamboats ....for the proselyting of a Theological Hypothesis that causes plenty of wrangle among Christians at home! Small wonder that Christianity meant so little in the Orient!

Instead of sending missionaries to convert the Japanese, or the Chinese, or the Hindu, to Christian ethics, we should import a few of those Orientals to bring Christian ethics across the seas to us. At least it seemed so, as I probed deeper and deeper into the activity I had gone out to survey.

I had not been in Japan a fortnight before my conscience began to hurt me. Dr. Taylor, Bishop Fisher, the others back at 150 Fifth Avenue in New York, had made this trip possible that I might become a polite propagandist for the missionary movement. Instead of this, my manifest conclusion was growing more embarrassing that the kindliest thing which we brain-strapped Christians could do would be to pack up our vaunted missionary enterprises and let the "heathen" alone. Coming right down to it—and my opinion did not alter when I finally sailed homeward—the "heathen" had far more to teach us than we could teach him in a millennium of Sundays. And I think my conclusion is the conclusion of every sane, unbiased, logical Nordic who has spent an appreciable time in the Orient. There are phases of oriental life that are merciless and vile. There is ignorance and super-stition, poverty and squalor. But have we not also the merciless and vile, the ignorant, the superstitious, among our western nations? Unkind tradesmen-residents often referred to such spiritual projects as I was surveying, as "the missionary racket." It was not such, by any means, as we know rackets in popular parlance. Long before I came to quit Japan, I labeled the movement "the missionary blunder." There is all the difference in the world between a racket and a blunder.

And yet invariably a queer sixth sense would whisper to me that I was emphatically not upon a pleasure jaunt. It had not happened by a lucky chance that Dr. Taylor had picked up one of my stories in a transcontinental train. Nor was I out there, moving among these teeming Asiatics to give thousands of earnest Christian people broken illusions about the efficacy of converting the "heathen" to our Christ. It was bigger than anything that I had stumbled upon to date. I was out there in preparation for something—that was it!—getting an education in international politics while I yet had time, seeing a world of international affairs that in my previous provincialism I had scarcely dreamed existed. I talked with Red Cross nurses, with Japanese officials. Gradually I became intimate with missionary problems, with the quandaries of Japanese statesmanship, with Nipponese psychology. My sympathy, understanding and tolerance for the Japanese people began to grow apace.

One rainy night in the Methodist auditorium in Karuizawa, the "Saratoga" of Japan far up in its interior, a tall, military personage intercepted me as we started back to the Iglehart camp. "Isn't your name Pelley?" I agreed that it was.

"I understand you're a writer for The Saturday Evening Post. My name's Phelps . . . George S. Phelps. I'm International Y. M. C. A. Secretary for the Far East with headquarters down in Tokyo. Your boats have been pulled off the China passenger service, Bishop Harris tells me, and you're sort of marooned here till the Intervention ends." Again I agreed, wondering what was coming.

"I'm here to find out if the `Y' could interest you in a proposition to go up to Siberia and do some special work . . . acting as a sort of scout for the establishment of the canteens we're going to install all through Russia. Also, being a trained newspaperman, you're equipped to take on certain espionage work that needs to be done . . . it'll give you the chance to see Russia under Bolshevism."

It seemed as though a great segment fell into proper place in those moments in my life.

I went back to the house and found Marion in a corner of the Iglehart living room with a big bag of knitting.

"I'm getting into the War," I told her simply. It was all in my brevet.

The future still held the key that unlocked that Higher Door, however, and I had nine more years of journeyings through lowlands and morasses before I knew my earthly commission, that Christos had not spoken falsely when He said, "In my Father's house are many mansions! I go to prepare a place for you, that where I am, ye may be also!"

I was the Alpha and Omega of earthly achievement. But only the heights of the world could expound it. I went down at last, climbing down painfully, step after step. A different set of muscles now shrieked with the torture.

Significant to relate, I went down alone. Always and forever, we go down alone.

My party of the night had all vanished now. Brilliance of sunlight was flooding the world. Yet the depths into which I was lowering myself, moment on moment, were dark, dark. I was heading into Bolshevia to know the Bath of Horror.

I was presently to go through ten to fifteen years of still more practical experiencing before I could perceive this education in perspective and properly appraise the merits of its factors. The night came in Yokohama when I kissed the wife of my youthful marriage goodbye and went aboard a sleeping car that would take me to Tsuruga, the seaport on Japan's western side where the Russian steamers docked and where troops were being loaded.

In the hour that followed I got my orders. The officials of the Young Men's Christian Association desired to secure vital information about internal Siberia and eastern Russia that would facilitate a drive to turn the young men of Russia away from satanic Leninism, to locate strong educational centers under Christian auspices from the cities of Kamchatka southwestward to the Ukraine, and conversely to acquaint the people of the United States with the true nature of Communism behind the scenes. It was a noble plan, and all honor be given to the men who then thought it possible. Could it have succeeded, the story of Siberian Asia might have been altered.

My orders amounted to this: "Go into the interior and find out what's happening. Make contact with so-and-so at this point, and so-and-so at that point. Wherever you can do so, bring us back Kodak pictures of conditions but don't let yourself be caught using a camera too boldly or it means you'll be shot. If scaled orders or documents are put into your hands to bring out for the diplomatic corps, bring them out and no ques-tions asked. You have carte blanche to move anywhere behind the Czech, the Japanese, and White Russian lines from Khabarovsk to Tomsk. You'll do this as an ordinary Red Triangle secretary, hitching your canteen car to Japanese and White Russian troop trains. No one is to know that you're anything else. And you'll start up-country into the Blagovyeshchenck sector, and around the Amur River district, day after tomorrow. When you reach Chita, wait there, if advisable, for contact with the official Red Triangle Commission that is going through Irkutsk in about a fortnight and make your first report." It was a strange commission.

No man in the whole war had a stranger one. I found out that I was combi-nation Red Triangle secretary, war correspondent, espionage agent, secret photographer, canteen proprietor, and consular courier—a sort of field scout for the advance guard of the Christian Y, striving to plant sanity, decency, and political stability in a land being slowly mutilated and mangled by Communism. In all of it I was to have no bodyguard, no official standing beyond my khaki uniform that carried the dubious military authority of second lieutenant. If I landed in a jam I could not appeal to my government for protection. Once I left Vladivostok, I must depend solely on my wits. If I came out, I would merely be thanked. If I did not come out, no one would be the wiser. I would be just another dead body staring up at the cold Siberian sun to be picked by the jackals that roamed the empty wastes.

Viewed in a more personal light, however, it meant a stupendous field for social and political observation. I had been handed an entire theater of Asiatic hostilities to research at caprice. I had such a chance as came to no other man in the war to apprise myself of racial and psychological conditions from Japan to Turkestan. I would see Bolshevism installed in a country with my own eyes—and the more creditable eye of the Kodak. I could meet and discuss this great soviet "experiment" and men who were undertaking to combat it tooth and claw in its incipient stages. Furthermore, I was to be a private military observer of Japanese troops maneuvers throughout Manchuria and North China. I was to live among the little brown men under war-time conditions. I was to meet up with ill-fated General Kolchak and his heroic White Russians, to become caught in the great eastern exodus of royalist refugees fleeing before the Latvian mercenaries of Lenin and Trotsky, and hear from them by first-hand contact exactly what had happened in Petrograd and Moscow—and even Ekaterinburg with its Romanoff shambles—as the vast Communistic regime came in.

When parlor socialists and drawing room pinks here in the United States try to tell me what Bolshevism is or is not, or what Communism will do or not do, I need not rely on Jewish propaganda or fanatical ignoramuses to serve me with the truth. I WAS THERE AND SAW COMMUNISM INSTALLED BEFORE MY GAZE!

I left Vladivostok on the day after that conference, and thereupon and until after the end of the war, I was to all intents and purposes a free-lance adventurer, my own private espionage agent, lost in the immensity of embattled Asia, gaining my own soldier-of-fortune education and enlightenment for the role I would be called upon to play in my own country fifteen years in the future. With such a background, such an opportunity, such an experience, such a training, how could I do otherwise than pursue my present calling?

The terrain was flat, sandy and overgrown with scrub. Hundreds of miles resembled the landscape between Fitchburg and Boston back in Massachusetts. Our locomotive burned wood. Showers of sparks had long since fired the woodlands far back from the tracks. Lakes and ravines opened as we mounted northward toward Kamchatka. Billions of wild flowers, of every conceivable color and variety, carpeted the uplands. The roadbed was rock-ballasted, the curves broad and stolid, the bridges heavy and substantial. But of cities and towns we saw next to none. The railroads in Siberia, not constructed for private profits from the citizenry but for movement of troops in war, made no effort to zigzag from community to community. Straight trackage was the rule, and if a city or town happened to be miles off the right-of-way, it was transportationally short on luck. The proximity of a sizable community might be indicated only by a long low railroad station, built half of logs, set back from the tracks across a rough-planked platform.

The buildings comprised everything from waiting room and freight depot to station-master's private home and the omnipresent hot-water house. Most of these units were painted flagrant mustard yellow. The typical Russian touch was supplied by the carved arabesque and rococo decorations in the angles of the gables.

Hour after hour, day after day, we droned northward, steadily approaching the Alexieffs' battlefields. Japanese troops were now everywhere in evidence, vigilant against guerrilla raidings. Bands of these renegade raiders made any sort of traveling precarious. Cossack groups, defected from the regular armies after the coming of Lenin, were plundering and pillaging on principle. In our car we had Josef, a Czech private, as cook and orderly. One night he summoned me excitedly and pointed northwestward. I summoned Vyles as quickly. The twilight sky held a horrid nimbus. Red flames were shooting higher as the railroad distance lessened.

"Some bonfire!" Vyles cried worriedly.

"Ah tank Blagovyeshchenck, she burn," muttered Josef. A city consumed by flames!

The train slowed down and proceeded cautiously, lit by the growing glare, darkness smothered with ominous suddenness. A man on a pony went tearing past. We could not tell his nationality but Josef addressed him in Bohemian Russian.

"He say Bolsheveek set fire. Mooch peeble shot. Japs have battle on hands preety qvick. Mebee beeg bridge down ahead, we wait here long time!

This disruption of the peasantry was a piteous thing. All Siberia, I was presently to learn, was a chaotic migration of disrupted peasantry, no destination to be arrived at, no geographical knowledge of the country to enable provincials to return to their villages—which all too often had become charred heaps of cabins on lonely steppes. Peasant trains were choked to suffocation when cold weather arrived with these peregrinating homesteaders. Whole villages of peasants would seize upon a train, get into it, and refuse to be ejected. Most of the trains had freight cars half as big again as those in the United States with wheels beneath the coaches, and rails beneath the wheels, and as sympathetic railroad crews manned cars and locomotives, these villages MOVED— so long as wood or coal held out. When it did not hold out, the engine crew would halt at a point on the steppes, go over the hill with portable barrows, and come back with surface coal turned up beneath the sod.

And what sights were all too common beneath the windows of those coaches! I know, I know!

Who can describe a Tatar battlefield piled or strewn with human bodies? The macabre sights, as Japanese or Czech troops set about interring the dead, if one could term it interment, were rendered thrice unspeakable by the stark nakedness of the corpses slowly bloating in putrefactive sunshine. Mangled bodies, burned bodies, bodies impaled by many things besides honest bayonets! The barbarous practice of stripping the dead of fabrics or boots, too valuable to bury, was something so common that it soon aroused no comment. Of the demoniacal mutilations I cannot write. But I made rakish discoveries in those horrible days. I learned that a corpse, left overlong above ground, turns a sickish green-black. I learned that the dead on a battlefield sometimes move, sometimes groan—without a spark of life

160

within them. A mysterious feature of those Siberian raiding fields was the unaccountable quantities of what seemed to be tar paper thrown promiscuously about in tattered sheets. What it was, where it came from, I never learned accurately. I made the discovery too that human stench can become so terrific that the sense of smell suspends, the nostrils no longer sense it. Few attempts were made to lift the charred corpses and bury them in shrouds. There were no shrouds. A trench was dug. Ropes were looped over stiffened members and piles of bodies dragged apart and across the sod as so much carrion . . . for dumping in such trenches. Certainly they made warfare as I saw it in Siberia. No man can say that he has lived a full life until he has known Love, Riches, and War. And the greatest of these is War.

Seeing a man shot before one's eyes was not half so terrible as those grinning, bloated things strewn around amid sheets and scraps of the unaccountable tar paper—which must have been from water-proof linings of munitions boxes. Again and again I thought to myself . . . "and once, not so many years ago, each and every one of them was a pink and gurgling infant whom some forgotten mother had suffered equally as frightfully to bring into this bedlamic world!" . . . At one time when our car was sidetracked within a fighting area a bewhiskered and hysterical Russian came running toward it. A volley from up the railroad yards got him. He slowed and staggered, hands clutching his belly. Presently he was sobbing, like a frightened little boy, one hand groping for the upright of a signal post, the other gripping at his groin where the lead bullet had gone in. When the raid was over, the little-boy sobbing gradually died away. So too did the life. When the train was suddenly jerked from the embattled district, his corpse was left lying against the post as though in his exertions he had merely dropped to sleep. It was usually a long time before anyone buried these corpses.

The country was bestrewn with such gruesome exhibits. I brought back one picture of five Czechs crucified against a rail fence. They had been there a week, dispatched by disemboweling. Bullets were too valuable to waste on executions.

And yet it was not the big major engagements, the mangling of the bodies, the dragging away of the women's one-time babies into trenches, the explosions under bridges and rolling stock, that stayed with me longest and in the accumulate indelibly inscribed that war in Siberia. It was the little human scenes of private distraction or tragedy that tore at the heartstrings and made the trek insufferable.

One rare October afternoon our car was shunted onto the end of a peasant train. A little family consisting of father, mother, three children and grandparents, came from the hamlet's crude log station and began to load into the car just ahead of us. I doubt if that family knew where it was going, but it was moving somewhere on principle. All its possessions were a sack of clothing, another of onions, a bucksaw and a sawbuck, and a three-legged stool. These were handed up. The grandparents got aboard and reached down for the children.

Then for some reason the young husband made a quick trip back into the station. The building had scarcely hidden him when the train started suddenly. "Papa! Papa!", wailed the distraught young mother who was still on the ground. Her parents and babies were being borne away from her and her husband could not hear her. In mad panic, unable to get aboard, she seized insanely on the door frame to exert her strength and hold that train back. Her fingers locked into it as in a death-clutch. "Stop it! Stop it!" she wailed in Russian. But the train did not stop. It gathered momentum and she presently lost her footing. In terrible danger of being crushed beneath the wheels, she was dragged down the track. "Papa! Papa! Help me!" she wailed. That "Help me!" rang in my ears for a month and a day. Finally her grip was ruthlessly ripped loose. She crumpled against a culvert.

Happily to report, it did not kill her. Happier to relate, the train was not departing out of that station. It had merely gone down the yards to back up upon a spur. So the children and parents were presently restored to that wracked young mother and the befuddled husband who lifted her tenderly. But no wail of the dying ever rang half so poignantly in my heart as the cry of love-fused maternity with which she greeted her parents and babies miraculously restored to her.

Human nature in the raw. Human love, human emotion, human heartbreak, human tragedy.... Nothing in these later years causes my temper to slip with greater ease than to hear some smug American fat-head declare what has taken place in Russia, "Oh, but those barbarians!—they naturally go in for riot and bloodshed! We're too civilized for such things to happen in America."

Day after day, week after week, I moved onward among these charmingly simple folk, characters out of Tolstoi, the prototypes in a thousand instances of my people up in New England, subscribers to The Evening Caledonian back in the Green Mountains. Generous to a fault, greeting us Americans with meats, butter, vegetables, refusing time after time to take a cent of payment, I remember them as gentle, inoffensive souls with a hurt look in their big and wistful eyes that any such scourge could have come upon their land. Dead now they are, most of them ....murdered, liquidated by the sword or starvation.

TO BE CONTINUED

FIRST CONTACT WITH ELDER BROTHER

(From The New Liberator, Oct. 1930, by W.D. Pelley)

I had been in a strange state of stupefaction, as it were, in the days immediately following my nocturnal experience in my bungalow. [See Seven Minutes in Eternity] I knew that I had been somewhere and met and talked in a baffling way with entities who the world would consider as "dead." And yet, to go out in the street and proclaim it would only get me branded as an idiot or liar. What had happened to me, so long as I had no way of checking up on it through others, or proving it to others in the developments of circumstance, must always remain as a personal experience, a personal illumination.

I had no mind to take anyone into my confidence about it. In fact, I came out of seclusion with the idea of keeping it forever to myself. I was too upset philosophically, from what I had seen and heard, to do much more than ponder upon it and try to assimilate its astounding significance.

True, something had happened to me physically as a result of it, because I had a small office staff of employees in a Pasadena business in which I was interested who immediately began exclaiming at some elusive alteration in my personal appearance. But autosuggestion, arrived at in sleep, might easily be responsible for such bodily enhancement, so I let them exclaim and applied myself to business.

Finally I decided to get away from California and go to New York. I wanted a perspective on myself and my environment — not to mention the possibility of talking with students of such phenomena and finding out whether or not they could give me interpretation of some phases of cosmology I seemed to have had relayed to me from the Other

Side which I believed I had visited. If other people had undergone similar visitations that checked up with mine in detail — as to procedure and the environment visited — then I might begin to credit that my cognizance of Reality had not been self-delusion. Once during an attack of typhoid fever, I had known the seeming reality of delusions and illusions and was not minded to hoax myself when my whole future career might depend on the validity of the episode.

The morning before starting for New York, however, a strange thing happened, which I have already mentioned in previous writings. I was standing in the living room of my bungalow with briar in one hand and tobacco tin in the other. As I started to fill my pipe, something struck the tobacco tin seemingly from beneath. The can spun an arc in the air just above my hands and spilled broadcast along the rug. Contiguous with this uncanny happening, I heard my first clairaudient voice. It said,

"Bill, give up your smoking!"

I looked at the spilled can lying near my feet and felt a weird thrill of fright. Later in the day, when I attempted to draw forth a package of cigarettes, I heard a repetition of the first beseechment. But this thing was notable: that following evening I commenced to have a strange aversion to the taste of tobacco. By the next morning all desire for it had gone and for the ensuing eight months I had not the slightest hunger for it in any form. I might interpolate here that one evening in Manhattan, eight months later, the same Voice that had appealed to me to give up my smoking carne to me in the same manner in the midst of a psychic message and instructed me to send out to the corner drugstore for a packet of cigarettes.

"We think you had better resume smoking," the instruction came. "It seems to open up your subconscious mind by relaxing your nerves and thus you are a better receiving organism. But don't dissipate in nicotine or we will kill the taste for it in you again!" I did as instructed and have been a moderate pipe smoker since.

Leaving Pasadena finally, enroute for New York, I was riding across New Mexico the second night out when my third dramatic experience occurred in the club car. I was alone in the club car about 10:30 at night. All the other passengers had gone back in their berths. Only the porter was present in the buffet getting his affairs closed up for the day. I had put a copy of Emerson in my bag and happened at the moment to be reading his "Over-Soul." I was not asleep, not even drowsy. The car clicked monotonously eastward, eastward.

Suddenly as I turned a page, something happened! I seemed to be bathed in a douche of pure white light on that moving Pullman. A great flood of Revelation came to me out of which a Voice spoke such as I had never heard before. What it said, I prefer to keep permanently to myself. But in that instant I knew that my bungalow experience had not been a dream, or even self-hallucination.

Particularly I knew of the reality of that Entity whom the world now designates as Jesus of Nazareth! I knew that He was not a mythical religious ideal. I knew His ministry and career had been a literal actuality and that I had once seen Him when He was thus in His flesh!

I make this statement guardedly and in full realization of its dramatic import. I knew in those moments in that empty club car that all the emotional reactions I had known during my life about Him up till then had not been delusions of grandeur, nor superiority complexes.

166

Jesus of Nazareth was not afar on some distant golden throne. He was here in a modern world of Pullmans and porters, radio and tabloids, chain shirt shops and talking movies.

I remained inert in that club car till long after the porter was snoring in his berth toward the front of the coach. When I got to my feet and went back to my own berth, I had an entirely new concept of my future activities.

This sounds, I know, like a Messianic Complex. Perhaps many a character since the Palestinian Incarnation of the Master, who has been able to give humanity a new interpretation of that Splendorful Personality, also can be dismissed into the Messianic-Complex classification. No matter! I knew what I knew! And I was calmly content from that night onward to let events take their course, for I had a strange feeling that all would be well if I but kept my pact. This, I might say, has come out literally in fact!

All that had happened, however, had happened to me privately. Still there was nothing that I could present to scientific-minded persons in proof of these two phenomenal episodes. Not that it was necessary to convince others. But all the same, having been a practical newspaperman with a practical newspaperman's outlook on strange fads and "isms", I had no mind to go skewed in my thinking and develop a crack in my reasoning brain.

I rode the rest of the way to New York not doing any reading, for reading was impossible. I watched the landscape in a stupefied daze.

Then, going across Indiana on the New York Central two days later, which happened to fall on a Sunday afternoon, I heard the Clairaudient Voice a third time.

Understand, it did not come to me at my own behest or invitation. On none of the previous occasions had I expected it. So now, when I had reached the place where I dared wonder consciously about the phenomenon in New Mexico, my thought was answered with an audible sentence.

Again it serves no purpose to tell what the question was which I was cogitating upon, or the answer I received. But it was a direct confirmation of the fact that there was a greater significance to my vivid concepts of Jesus throughout childhood and adolescence than mere delusions or Messianic complexes.

I got to New York as a man appalled by what was occurring to him and the work which I seemed bidden to do in interpreting phases of Messianic doctrine which up to that time had been as abstruse to me as to any purblind ecclesiastic. But the last thought in my mind was to tell anyone of these private communications, or make any claims about having contact with the Entities I was being forced to credit from overpowering contact. Neither did I expect at that time that events in circumstance would begin to bear out these prognostications which appalled me.

I got a room at the Commodore and called a lady friend whom I knew to be almost an adept in psychical research and a particularly devout and lovely soul. I apprised her of my being in town and asked if I could visit her in her apartment that evening. The phone conversation ended by her promising to come to the hotel and have dinner with me first.

I kept the appointment. But here again, I got the outward evidence of queer things afoot when she confronted me in the Commodore's foyer. Her face went blank. She exclaimed,

"For pity's sake, what's happened to you! You're not the same man who went to California a few months ago!"

I smiled away her temporary wonderment and we had our dinner. She persistently questioned me about my experiences since we had last seen one another. Finally, out in the ladies' lounge, I was trapped into telling her of my nocturnal experience.

"My dear boy", were her well-remembered words, "you got out of your body — unhinged something — and went somewhere."

"How do you know?", I demanded.

"In the first place," she said, "the technique of the whole experience checks up perfectly with similar experiences which hundreds of other persons are constantly having. Secondly, I'm psychically aware at this moment of a discarnate entity of particularly beautiful character standing near your shoulder and giving me interpretations of it in complete impressions which I understand perfectly."

"You mean I actually died, that night in Altadena, but returned after death to my physical body?" "Something of the sort. Have you ever done any automatic writing?"

"I've heard of it in a vague way," I said. "But I never saw it actually performed."

"Let's go up to my apartment," she suggested. "Let's prepare to take an automatic message and see if anything confirmatory happens."

A half-hour later we were settled in a beautiful room in the West Fifties with a cheery fire going in the grate and the New York noises shut out by heavy curtains. My friend had drawn a small taboret table over close to her knees. Now she invited me to sit down on the divan at her right, beside her. Sharpened pencils and a generous pad of paper had been provided. She turned back the cuff on her right wrist and bade me grasp her hand just below her palm.

"Hold it tightly," she instructed, as though to keep me from writing, "but leave your elbow working freely so that my whole hand and arm in conjunction with yours can make swinging penmanship."

I did so. She rested the sharpened pencil point on the pad and leaned back in easy relaxation. Suddenly our two hands started to move in unison. The pencil before us began making rhythmic swings and circles!

It seemed at first as though my lady friend was deliberately making the geometric figures which followed with acceleration as our combined grasp became more and more elastic. Then to my amazement, a long, round, flowing script began to form beneath the pencil, reaching the end of the line and coming back with a flourish to begin a new one. This was what was written :

"Memory is not memory if we must make new thought-bodies when we give up our material bodies. Man will some day know the truth and then we will make real bodies in the image of God. Make no mistake, we are those who are now in the light and we have much to tell you. 'Music of the Spheres' is no idle phrase but the very center of the mystery of the creation of this, your universe!

"Where there is Harmony, there is Life, and all discord is Death. We of the more harmonious plane, which is next above the plane of earth, make this statement to you because you are of that company whose bodies are yet of earth but whose eyes are opened to the perception of the Truth. Many of us are with you, not only at this moment, but in many moments when you are unaware of our presence. We will endeavor to make more power for you in all that you undertake if you will endeavor to open yourselves more completely to our touch."

That was all! Wait as we would, no more writing appeared on the pad. Yet I knew both from the bodily position of my hostess, as well as from my own grip on her wrist, that she could not have consciously fabricated and written what lay before us on the paper. Moreover, there was so much we both wanted to know, that had it been a subconscious effort, we most certainly would have gone on writing for an indefinite period.

Nothing happened all the next day. But I was back in my psychic friend's apartment promptly at 7:30 the ensuing evening, prepared to try the strange writing again. All this time no other manifestations of the clairaudient voice had come to me personally beyond those reported.

Promptly when we got into working posture that next night, however, the sharpened pencil point started off with vigor. Following is the literal lengthy message we got on the second evening of our

171

experimenting, without a word or punctuation mark changed. I might say that I carefully preserved every scrap of paper, and for almost two years have taken care of every word of Intelligence which has come over thus — or in any sitting at which I have been present — transcribing it carefully and filing it for future reference. [see the Master Message, Call Me Not Master]

SPEECH TO HISTORICAL SOCIETY

(Speech honoring Mr. Pelley delivered by Mel Pearson to the Hamilton County Historical Society, August 17, 1997)

Thank you for that nice introduction.

Right at the outset I want to thank you for inviting me to make a presentation about my father-in-law, William Dudley Pelley. He was and is a controversial figure as we all know, and members of the family are always happy to have the opportunity of clearing up some of the misunderstandings, misrepresentations and distortions that surround his life.

I also want to state that I am happy and comfortable to be part of this law enforcement history program. Over the years Mr. Pelley and his family had many contacts with law enforcement personnel and generally we found them to be professional in their conduct and people of integrity. Mr. Pelley had a special relationship with the U. S. marshals, especially in Washington, D. C. They had mutual respect for each other. I remember a Captain Kidwell of the District of Columbia law enforcement personnel who wrote a letter to the Parole Board stating that they never considered Mr. Pelley an inmate, but considered him an associate. That was a pretty good relationship.

I will try to be as brief as I can so as to leave room for questions and answers. I find such exchange is always more productive than simply listening to a speaker.

I might note right at the outset that when Mr. Pelley moved to Noblesville in 1940, one of the local papers, reflecting quite a flagrant point of view that existed throughout the land, stated that there were four major roads out of the city and Pelley and his ilk were invited to depart on any one of them. Some ten years later, when he was released from prison, he was invited to speak at one of the Service Clubs and the report one heard was that the listeners found Mr. Pelley a most intriguing and charming individual. Later the Ledger dispatched a reporter who visited with Mr. Pelley for a whole afternoon and the paper then carried a front page feature article as to his background and publishing. At a later time I had occasion to talk to the then chief of police, Mr. Shoat. He characterized Mr. Pelley as just a "radical Republican."

Time does have a way of healing, and increased knowledge has a way of eliminating prejudices and changing people's viewpoints.

In order to be brief I will divide Mr. Pelley's full life into three areas:

First, there are his literary achievements which led him to get national recognition as a short story writer and novelist.

Second, there are the years primarily during the 1930s when Mr. Pelley was engaged in his economic and political writings which, of course, made him so controversial. It was also the time of his legal difficulties when he was arrested, convicted of the political crime of "sedition", making him perhaps the outstanding political prisoner of this century.

Third, after his release from federal prison in 1950 after serving seven and a half years, Mr. Pelley spent the remainder of his life until he passed away in 1965 writing metaphysical books and publishing several esoteric magazines.

Let us now consider each of these major sections of Mr. Pelley's life:

His literary career: Most people are quite astounded to find that Mr. Pelley had over 250 short stories published in the best magazines of the time. They appeared in Saturday Evening Post, Redbook, Colliers and other so-called slick magazines. He was a constant contributor to The American Magazine.

He won the "O. Henry Memorial Award" for the best short story in the nation for two different years. Several times his stories appeared among the best short stories of the year as edited by Edward J. O'Brien.

Along with his short stories he managed to write a half dozen novels, two of which were made into movies. One book was the "Fog" which was published by Little Brown and Co. and sold nearly a half million copies. The other book was called "Drag". This took him to Hollywood where he was scenario writer for a number of movies.

He became acquainted with many of the stars of that day, such as Mary Pickford, Gloria Swanson, William Boyd and others. His closest friend was Lon Chaney who many of you may remember starred in the

"Hunchback of Notre Dame." My wife, Adelaide [Pelley's daughter], tells of his lifting her onto his lap, placing a couple of chocolate cup wrappers in his eyes and making a little horror show for her alone.

It was because of his writing achievements that high dignitaries of the Methodist Church contracted Mr. Pelley to travel around the world to make an assessment of foreign missions. When he arrived in Japan, Bolshevism was taking over Russia and the United States had joined with other countries in what was known as the Siberian Intervention. Mr. Pelley dropped his writing assignment, joined the American forces, was given a military ranking of second lieutenant, and traveled some 5,000 miles into Russia on the Siberian railway where he witnessed firsthand the bloody takeover of Communism.

The experience left an indelible scar on his mind and soul and was to have much influence in his later stand against the recognition of Stalinist Russia during the 1930s. .

Up to this time Mr. Pelley had not engaged himself in political writings of any kind. However, that was to drastically change. It came about when the studio he was working for gave him the writing assignment on a short that was being made for the State Department. This took him to Washington where he became a close friend of Bob Sharp of the Secret Service who was really his boss when he was traveling in Russia. He also became a good friend of Dr. Strath Gordon who was at one time the head of the British Secret Service. These two men, along with Congressman Louis T. McFadden, who was chairman of the House Banking committee, were alarmed with what was transpiring in the U. S. in the way of destroying the independence of the American people.

While Communism was being forced on the Russian people by terror and murder, a much more subtle thing was happening in America. It was a process of "government by reaction". Powerful economic and financial entities were creating the severe economic and financial conditions making it natural for government to step in with all of its relief and subsidy programs, all to the end of the people losing their independence. It created condition of one-third of the people ill-fed, ill-clothed and ill-housed. Over 15 million people were unemployed.

Pelley was moved to drop all his lucrative fictional writing and commence exposing what was transpiring. Central to his effort was opposing the United States recognition of Stalinist Russia. It was to no avail. He also wrote most strongly of the steps that were leading the United States into war. His strong belief, along with those who made up the "America First Committee", who had such prominent supporters as Charles Lindbergh, was that the United States should remain neutral and thus could be a real influence for peace after the European countries worked hard to destroy themselves.

It was during this time that Mr. Pelley wrote a book called No More Hunger which outlined economic and political change that would unleash the nation's full productive capability, implement all basic human rights, and would create a nation free of debt and violence. To promote the change that he advocated he brought into being an organization called the Silver Legion. Unfortunately, the members became known as Silver Shirts and this made it easy for those who wanted to suppress Mr. Pelley's thinking to unfairly link the organization to European shirt organizations.

Incidentally, I am presenting you with a copy of "No More Hunger" and a copy of a companion book that I recently wrote called "There Is A Way!"

Our entrance into World War II set the stage for Mr. Pelley being arrested in 1942 and charged with violating the wartime sedition act, called the Espionage Act of 1917. It was but routine to get a conviction. Since we were allied with Russia, all Mr. Pelley's anti-communist writings were presented as undermining the loyalty of the American soldier in our combined leadership. He was denied all his basic constitutional rights of due process for subpoenaing witnesses and presenting evidence. Congressman Thorkelson of Montana and Charles Lindbergh were the only prominent people allowed to testify in Mr. Pelley's defense, and their testimony was severely limited.

Prominent constitutional attorneys who became interested in Mr. Pelley's trial and conviction exclaimed openly that he had been crucified. But those intent on silencing Mr. Pelley weren't satisfied. Within the year of his 15-year sentence, Mr. Pelley was shackled and taken to Washington, D. C. to be included in the Mass Sedition Trial. Some 30 writers and publishers, all opposed in varying degrees to the Administration's economic and war policies, were indicted on a basis of conspiracy to violate the peacetime sedition Act called the Smith Act.

Both the Espionage Act of 1917 and the Smith Act had the same provisions. The same evidence that was used against Mr. Pelley in Indianapolis was now introduced at the Mass Sedition Trial. This was a flagrant violation of the constitutional provision of "double jeopardy" prohibiting any person from being twice tried for the same offense.

After the prosecution had spent several million dollars, making special trips to Germany trying to link the defendants to Nazism and failing to collect any real evidence, Chief Justice Laws of the District Court in Washington, D. C., dismissed the whole case by stating that it would be a "travesty on justice to permit the case to go on any longer." The defendants had endured six years of being charged with an unprovable case.

Books have been written as to the illegality of the sedition charges against the 30 defendants, including Mr. Pelley, but I would like to quote from an editorial in the Washington Times-Herald written by it chief editorial writer, Frank C. Waldrop called "The Cheapest Act". [quote omitted to save space here]

So ended the infamous Mass Sedition Trial. It seemed but routine to get a reversal on Mr. Pelley's conviction in Indianapolis in 1942. Mr. Pelley's attorney immediately filed a writ of habeas corpus in the Federal District Court of Indianapolis. The basis of the writ was to cite the three important Supreme Court Decisions that were the basis of Judge Law's dismissal of the Mass Sedition Case, and were made subsequent to Mr. Pelley's conviction in Indianapolis. The three cases were:

1) The Viereck case in which the Supreme Court reversed the conviction because of the inflammatory and prejudicial language used by the federal prosecutors. In Mr. Pelley's case the prosecutors had inflamed the jury by likening him to Benedict Arnold and a traitor to his nation.

2) The Baumgartner case in which the Supreme Court underscored First Amendment Rights, that they weren't shelved just because of involvement in war.

3) The third case and the most important was the Hartzell Case which the Supreme Court reversed citing the two basic elements that must 'e present in order to get a sustainable conviction. Those elements were:

a) An element of intent which meant that the defendant intended to cause the harm that was being prevented by the statute.

b) An element of clear and present danger which meant the actions of the defendant did bring about the harm stated by the statute.

As soon as the Writ of Habeus Corpus was filed in Indianapolis, attorneys for the Justice Department filed a brief stating that the Indianapolis Court, despite the fact that it was the court of original trial, did not have jurisdiction because Mr. Pelley was physically in Washington where he had been held during the Mass Trial.

Immediately Mr. Pelley's attorney filed a similar Writ of Habeus Corpus in the Washington Court and, incredible as it might seem, attorneys for the Justice Department filed a brief contending that the Washington Court didn't have jurisdiction because, although Mr. Pelley was physically in Washington, he was only there technically by the court order of a writ of habeus corpus ad prosequendam.

The Justice Department had so arranged Mr. Pelley's confinement that they had succeeded in denying him one of his most sacred constitutional rights, and that is access to the courts. Where is due process when you don't have any court that will hear your pleading?

What about the constitutional provision that the writ of habeus corpus shall not be suspended?

Since I was president of the Justice for Pelley Committee it was suggested by our attorney that I approach the Justice Department and see if they would join in a stipulation agreeing that one of the courts must have jurisdiction. I presented the idea to a Mr. Morris, who was an assistant to the Attorney General of the United States, and I experienced what is properly called "arrogance of power". He looked at me and said, "Who in the hell do you think you are? I must tell you, we are resorting to dilatory tactics and we'll resort to all the damn dilatory tactics we want to!"

I responded just as adamantly that he wasn't even aware of his oath of office to protect and defend the laws of the land by deliberately denying a citizen his constitutional right of access to the courts and due process. And the Department of Justice was consistent in its arbitrary actions.

We, of course, filed a writ of certiorari with the Supreme Court, which was in due time denied. At the same time I contacted John O'Donnell, columnist for the Washington Times-Herald and the New York News. In his column, "Capitol Stuff" he wrote the following: (quote omitted to save space here)

It should be noted that Mr. Pelley was entitled to be released on parole after serving one-third of his sentence if he had a good behavior record. His behavior record was outstanding. At Terre Haute he not only conducted a Great Book program for the prisoners, but he wrote speeches for the warden and directed the putting together of a pictorial book of the Terre Haute Penitentiary which was considered to be the model institution in the nation. On one of my trips to Washington I visited the Bureau of Prisons building and had the opportunity to look over the book which was on a pedestal in the main entrance. When Mr. Bennett, head of the Bureau of Prisons, found that I was present, he took time to tell me how much they appreciated the professional job Mr. Pelley had done in putting together the book. In the Washington District Jail he reorganized the check-in system of the new prisoners, earning the gratitude of the U. S. Marshals by saving them hours of waiting.

The matter of jurisdiction was resolved by the Justice Department moving Mr. Pelley back to the Federal Penitentiary in Terre Haute.

Let it suffice to state that all the legal actions to get the Indianapolis conviction reversed met with no success. Each court contended that his case had been adjudicated. With his release on parole, spearheaded by the efforts of Senator Langer of North Dakota, Mr. Pelley was finally released and there was little reason to pursue costly legal action any further. At its best a favorable action by a court would simply confirm that Mr. Pelley had only been a political prisoner.

An interesting thing to note is that when I contacted former Senator Jim Watson of Indiana, whom I understand was this state's most powerful political figure in Washington, he immediately sent a letter to Judge Baltzell who had presided at Mr. Pelley's trial, and asked him to write a letter to the Parole Board asking for Mr. Pelley's release. Mr. Watson gave me the letter he received from Baltzell which stated that the sentencing judge had only meant to keep Mr. Pelley in prison during the duration of World War II.

On Valentine's Day, February 14, Mr. Pelley arrived back in Noblesville where he was to remain until his death in 1965. During those years he busied himself in writing many metaphysical books and organizing the other writings which covered many years. A complete set of 12 volumes were finished and he wrote a number of books making up a total list of over 20 volumes which he called the Soulcraft philosophy. At the same time during those years we published several esoteric magazines, one of which had a four-color cover. Our mailing was of such volume as to increase the rating of the local post office.

The legacy left by Mr. Pelley has nothing to do with his activities dealing with governmental abuses, the exploitive operations of economic and financial corporate giants, or even his efforts toward peace with his opposition to Stalinist communism. The real legacy is two-fold:

First, his blueprinting of a New Economic Order, which he called "The "Christian Commonwealth", which if embraced by the people would unleash the full productive potential of this nation, provide for an abundant life for every solitary individual, and build a nation of true economic justice devoid of debt and violence.

The second legacy is his writing of over 20 volumes presenting a working philosophy of life which he called "Soulcraft", or craft of the soul, which has helped tens of thousands of people over the years to find ballast and meaning in their lives in an ever-increasingly violent and unstable world.

Mr. Pelley clearly stated that the Soulcraft philosophy was not meant as a substitute for anyone else's religion. It was only meant to enhance a person's own particular religious persuasion.

Mission Statement

Give the truth to the world. Let it be received where it will. Many will read the messages. Some will accept the truth, others will read through curiosity, a few will ridicule. Yet to all is the truth given, and to all remains the power of choice.

The hope of the world in these times is in spiritualizing all forms of activity---promoting understanding through love and service. These must be the watchwords if the world is to come into lasting peace. We are trying to influence a world that is going astray and could cause undreamed of suffering. We are trying to overcome the thought of materialists and to bring a spiritual outlook into the earthly life. We need the help of all on earth who can think in spiritual terms. The great battle to be fought now is between the spiritual and the material, between idealism and carnalism. You can help by spreading the word---we are asking that you help because the battle may be long and the victory far away.

Halls of Light is not allied with any sect, denomination, political entity, organization, neither endorses nor opposes any cause. There are no dues for membership. Halls of Light is self-supporting through its own voluntary contributions. Halls of Light has but one purpose: to help through encouragement and understanding...

To contact the publishers or to obtain copies of our other books, please contact us at:

Email: goldtown11@gmail.com

Web: https://whoamiandwhyamihere.com/shop/

Other Books by TNT Publishing

Who am I and Why Am I here?

The Significance of Existence

Death and the Incredible Life After

Fear of Death Removed

Paradise Regained

Spiritual Laws Revealed

Unseen Forces

Too Good to Be True

The Truth of Life in the Spirit World

He Who Has Ears

The Great Awakening, Volumes I thru VII

The Great Awakening, Volume VIII,
THE WHITE STAR OF THE EAST

The Great Awakening, Volume IX,
I THE LORD GOD SAY UNTO THEM

The Great Awakening, Volume X,
MINE INTERCOM MESSAGES FROM THE REALMS OF LIGHT

The Great Awakening, Volume XI,
THE BOOK OF THE LORD

The Great Awakening, Volume XII thru XV,
TEMPLE TEACHINGS FROM THE HIGHER REALMS

Transfiguration Volumes I thru Volume VIII

The Part of Counsel

The Book of Wisdom

The School of Melchezedek

Hail! Hail! Unto the Victors

The Book of Light

The Book of Life

The Golden Scripts

Seven Minutes in Eternity

No More Hunger

Contact us at

Email: goldtown11@gmail.com

Web: https://whoamiandwhyamihere.com/shop/

www.ingramcontent.com/pod-product-compliance
Lightning Source LLC
Chambersburg PA
CBHW071531040426
42452CB00008B/967

* 9 7 8 1 7 3 7 3 0 7 1 2 9 *